Antiques

2W

THE LIBRARY OF ENGLISH ART

GENERAL EDITOR: C. M. WEEKLEY

# ENGLISH FURNITURE

## THE LIBRARY OF ENGLISH ART

### ENGLISH WATER-COLOURS
LAURENCE BINYON, C.H.
*Sometime Keeper of Prints and Drawings, British Museum*

### ENGLISH POTTERY AND PORCELAIN
W. B. HONEY
*Sometime Keeper, Department of Ceramics, Victoria & Albert Museum*

### ENGLISH DOMESTIC SILVER
CHARLES OMAN
*Keeper of the Department of Metalwork, Victoria & Albert Museum*

### ENGLISH FURNITURE
JOHN GLOAG, F.S.A.
*Author of 'The English Tradition in Design', 'A Short Dictionary of Furniture'.*
*'Guide to Furniture Styles: English and French', etc.*

### ENGLISH GLASS
W. A. THORPE
*Author of 'A History of English and Irish Glass', etc.*
*Sometime Deputy Keeper in the Victoria & Albert Museum*

### ENGLISH PORTRAIT MINIATURES
GRAHAM REYNOLDS
*Keeper in the Victoria & Albert Museum*

SOME BOOKS BY JOHN GLOAG

# ENGLISH FURNITURE

BY

## JOHN GLOAG

F.S.A., Hon. F.R.I.B.A., Hon. F.S.I.A.

SIXTH EDITION, REVISED
With 41 plates and 137 illustrations in the text

ADAM & CHARLES BLACK
LONDON

FIRST EDITION 1934
SECOND EDITION 1944    REPRINTED 1946
THIRD EDITION 1948
FOURTH EDITION 1952
FIFTH EDITION (revised and enlarged) 1965
SIXTH EDITION (revised with additions) 1973

ISBN  0 7136 1318 1

MADE IN GREAT BRITAIN
PRINTED BY R. & R. CLARK LTD. EDINBURGH

Scroll-ended bookcase on ball feet, japanned black with gilt decoration.
*Circa* 1810-15. Regency prototype of the Victorian ladies' chair:
japanned black with gilt brass gadrooned moulding on seat and back
frame. The material used for the upholstery is modern.

Dear Gordon,

　　　My admiration for you and all that you stood for, prompted me to dedicate this book to you when it was first published in 1934. During the years that have since passed, you have, through your personal work as a designer, as Director of the Council of Industrial Design, and as an inspired teacher, improved the character of contemporary furniture, and demonstrated the vitality of the English tradition in design.

John Gloag

1971

## INTRODUCTION TO THE SIXTH
## EDITION

THIS book, first published in 1934, is not a technical work, nor is it a manual for collectors of antique furniture. The chapters are intended to describe, and the illustrations to show, how the design of English furniture has, since the late fifteenth century, reflected changes in national taste. Good proportions are more important than mere age: a truth too often forgotten since the cult of collecting old furniture began to attract more and more devotees during the nineteenth century. The opening chapters sketch the historical background of design; chapters III to VII describe the evolution of different types of furniture, relating changes in design and decoration to architecture—the basic source of inspiration in every period, as furniture has seldom developed in isolation. The last three chapters, VIII, IX and X, were rewritten for the fifth, revised and enlarged edition published in 1965. Various amendments and additions have been made to the present edition, and some fresh illustrations in cluded in the text and plates. Eleven pages of drawings by the late E. J. Warne, that appeared in previous editions, have been retained.

JOHN GLOAG

1971

# CONTENTS

xi

# LIST OF PLATES

*Coloured frontispiece*

REGENCY SCROLL-ENDED BOOKCASE AND LADIES' CHAIR

## ACKNOWLEDGEMENTS

Drawings by the late E. J. Warne appear on pages
45, 49, 55, 59, 63, 65, 83, 87, 91, 97, and 103. The
source of all the other illustrations is acknowledged in
the captions.

The Cabinet-Maker's shop, 1830. Reproduced from the frontispiece of
the fifth edition of *The Cabinet-Maker's Guide, or Rules and Instructions
in the art of varnishing, dying, staining, japanning, polishing, lackering
and beautifying Wood, Ivory, Tortoiseshell, and Metal*, by G. A. Siddons.
(Published by Sherwood, Gilbert and Piper, 1830.) In the Introduction, the author observed that his was perhaps 'the only work that may
properly be called a Manual of the Arts, and the rapid sale which it met
with, is a proof of the estimation in which it was held . . .'

Mid-fifteenth-century oak seat in St. Mary's Hall, Coventry. This was probably the right-hand part of a triple seat which stood on the daïs of the Great Hall. The Hall was built in the early part of the century for the united guilds of St. Mary, St. John the Baptist and St. Catherine. The ornament used is characteristic of contemporary Gothic architecture. Reproduced from *Furniture with Candelabra and Interior Decoration*, by Richard Bridgens (London, 1838).

xvi

## CHAPTER I

# THE HISTORICAL BACKGROUND OF DESIGN
## 1500–1700

BEFORE considering the history of English furniture-making, the mind should be cleared of romantic prejudices. Nothing that is ugly in its form or inept or clumsy in its construction should be respected simply because it is an 'antique'. The study of antique furniture design is interesting and instructive if it is undertaken as a research into the methods of skilled and extraordinarily patient men who solved technical problems and were inventive with a limited range of materials. But if such study is undertaken in what can only be described as a spirit of antiquarian adoration, if reverence for mere age debilitates appreciation for good proportion, then it degenerates into 'collecting' in the worst magpie sense. The aesthetic integrity of the 'collection' that results from these sentimental raids into the past of furniture-making is based on the fact of age, as facts are understood by antique dealers. The collector to whom dates have become more vital than design is beginning to part with his critical faculty. Mr. Aldous Huxley dealt, not unjustly, with the situation that arises from this state of mind when he wrote: 'A man can paint beautiful pictures in a slum, can write poetry in Wigan; and conversely he can live in an exquisite house, surrounded by masterpieces of ancient art, and yet (as one sees almost invariably when collectors of the antique, relying for once on their own judgement, and not on tradition, "go in for" modern art) be crassly insensitive and utterly without taste'.[1]

Our furniture betrays our ideas to posterity in even greater detail than our architecture. People in the nineteen-thirties who furnished their houses with genuine (or imitation) antiques were illustrating for the benefit of the year 2000 the flight from realities that was then so characteristic of political, economic and social life. They dived into the past for comfort; so did statesmen. The people who furnished with stark, mechanistic design in steel revealed the revolutionary tendencies of the intelligentsia. Such furniture of basic structural lines was supposed to represent a complete break with tradition. Actually it represented nothing of the kind, for unless human beings alter their physical proportions (by ceasing to be vertebrates or mammals, for instance), their bodies make certain unchanging demands upon furniture. The slinging of fabric from a frame to form the back and seat of a chair was an old idea even in the sixteenth and seventeenth centuries, when leather and wood were used. Now tubular steel and leather or fabric are used; and thin steel frames were used in the eighteen-sixties and seventies in England and France. Chromium plating and the mechanical manipulation of tubes gave fresh variations to this form of furniture: nothing more.

In the past English furniture has always revealed the foibles of patrons and the limitations and enthusiasms of craftsmen and designers. The education of taste, the improvement or decline of manners and the

[1] *Along the Road*, Part II.

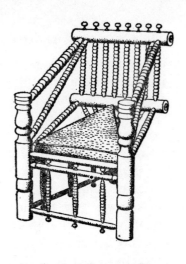

*Left*: Pew end with blind tracery, *circa* 1500, showing the influence of Perpendicular Gothic forms. From Steeple Aston: reproduced from Parker's *Glossary* (1845). *Right*: Turned chair of East Anglian origin, *circa* 1600. In the Fitzwilliam Museum, Cambridge. (Drawn by Ronald Escott.)

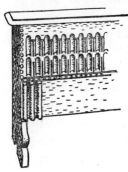

*Left*: Gouge carving, used to ornament flat surfaces in the late sixteenth century. *Right*: Gadrooning or nulling. (See upper part of bulbous supports of press cupboard on Plate VII.)

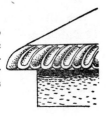

*Left*: Mid-seventeenth century single chair, with arched back rails carved with scrolls, split balusters decorating the back uprights. (See Fig. 20, page 55, also Plate XII.) *Right*: Examples of bobbin and spiral turning. (See Figs. 26 and 27, page 55, Fig. 38, page 63, and Plates IX, X, and XII.)

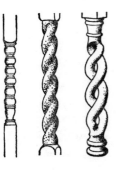

extravagance or sobriety of costume have all left indelible marks upon the shape and decoration of the things that have been made in wood since 1500.

Home life in Britain has enjoyed two long periods of urbane expansion in the past: one of them lasted for nearly four hundred years, and the other for just over two hundred, and they were separated by eleven centuries of comparative barbarism. The first was when Britain was part of the Roman Empire; the second began when Inigo Jones started to design buildings, and ended in the eighteen-thirties. We are just a century away from the end of the last period. The external results of those periods of security and civilised development were similar. Possibly because there is more in Bernard Shaw's figure of Britannus in *Caesar and Cleopatra* than a figure of fun. The character of Britannus, the ancient Briton with the soul of a Victorian maiden aunt, implies that geography has something to do with preserving national character. What we know of those two periods suggests that something in the land preserves the same ideas of comfort and propriety, the same gifts and tastes, which, stimulated by prosperous security, combine to create a quiet welcoming domestic architecture and the sort of homes no other land can match.

The first period left no legacies in architecture. The rudimentary civilisation that followed it inherited ruins; for when the plenty and order of the Roman Province of Britain were destroyed by the barbarian invasions the destruction was complete. The Saxon and Jutish soldiers stamped their muddy feet over the mosaic pavements of the well-planned, centrally-heated houses of the Roman citizens of Britain, hacked at a statue or a column to try the strength of their weapons, even as the barbarian conqueror of Constantinople centuries later smashed the column of serpents in the hippodrome with his mace. Soldiers on active service are always the same, whether they are casually butchering an Archimedes because he doesn't stand up smartly to attention when spoken to, or stabling their horses in a chapel to the detriment of a masterpiece of painting that adorns one of its walls, or shelling a cathedral with long-range guns. The old military desire to travel light caused the Saxon savages to burn what they could not conveniently loot; and in blood the dark ages began, and in blood they continued until the half-light of mediaeval civilisation preceded the Renaissance.

It was centuries before craftsmen gained the opportunity to round off the corners of the very rugged life that even the wealthy and powerful classes endured. All constructive and creative effort was diverted to church-building. In the castles and fortified manor houses furniture was elementary. Noblemen sat on benches, stools and chests, shivering in their furs, their eyes smarting as the fire in the great hall swirled smoke up to the roof. A chair was a rarity; a bed was a housing scheme for insects. Mediaeval furnishing seldom advanced beyond boxes and stools in their most elementary shapes; and although *the box and the stool are the basic forms of all furniture*, no skilled manipulation of those forms came to the service of comfort until the beginning of the sixteenth century. In the Middle Ages, luxury meant the addition of fabrics to the rigid shapes of furniture. Fabrics were hung around beds, draped over stools and tables, and hung on walls. Only when chairs with X-shaped frames were invented did fabrics become

*5*

structurally associated with furniture, through the craft of the coffer maker.[1]

The structural rigidity of the Middle Ages haunted furniture design and furnishing until the maturity of that second period, which was even more Roman in taste and form than the Romano-British period itself, the English Renaissance. From 1660 until 1830 England enjoyed a period of unexampled harmony in the design of everything connected with the making, decorating and furnishing of houses. But the harmonious adjustment of all these various branches of design took time. There was a preliminary period of aesthetic anarchy. In that period craftsmen were bewildered. They were the victims of a new and fashionable form of education. They were not themselves subjected to it; they merely felt its effect upon their lords and masters, the new well-travelled noblemen of the Renaissance.

Henry VII, who was one of the first modern statesmen, had pacified England and made it fit for traders rather than heroes to live in. The reserves of treasure which he accumulated were spent royally by that more than royal figure Henry VIII, and it was under Henry VIII that the new Renaissance nobility began to collect ideas from abroad and to make those experiments in reading, in music, and in decorative art which disrupted English tradition, and destroyed the satisfying simpli-

---

[1] The X-shaped chair frame was a re-discovery rather than an invention. Such chairs were used in Egypt over a thousand years before the Christian era. In a tomb painting in the British Museum (No. 10016) there is an X-shaped stool with a deer seated thereon. This occurs in a satirical composition of animals taking the place of human beings at a feast (New Kingdom). A copy of a tomb painting by Mrs. de Garis Davies in the British Museum (from the tomb of Huy, Thebes No. 40, *circa* 1360 B.C.) shows an X-shaped stool; the subject of the painting is Nubian princes bringing trinkets.

city of other work in stone, in wood and in iron. There were almost as many changes in the social outlook and structure in England between the opening of the sixteenth century and the peak of Elizabethan prosperity as there were between the middle of the eighteenth century and the turbulent individualism of prosperous Victorian industry. In all these social and economic changes the ruling classes had the fun because they set the fashions, and the men who worked with their hands, the craftsmen and the artisans, had their lives darkened by perplexity and, as the moral standards of the Middle Ages faded, by poverty.

They were perplexed because something external was thrust upon them which they did not wholly understand; something called 'fashionable taste' which was invented abroad, admired by well-travelled gentlemen, and imported. Furniture did not escape from its modish influence, and in the Elizabethan period furniture grew bloated in form and was restlessly decorative. It is not always apprehended that the Elizabethan period was one of those unfortunate phases of economic and social life in England when wealth outran education, when a new rich class, although its artistic appreciation for literature and music was profound, had not yet acquired the restraint which enabled it to appreciate good proportions and shapes and surfaces untroubled by ornamentation. The furniture that was made between 1570 and 1620 was for the most part as barbarous in form and repellently profuse in decoration as the furniture that was made between 1840 and 1910. The workmanship was not yet debauched. Bad though the designs were, the late Elizabethan and Jacobean furniture was well made. Copy books that illustrated the classic orders of

7

architecture came from Swiss, German and Flemish presses. The *Architectura* by J. Vredeman de Vries was issued in Antwerp in 1563, followed in 1566 by his *Compartimenta*, while from Nuremberg came a sinister and misleading work, Wendel Dietterlin's *Architectura*. Such popular architectural guides gave the classic orders and classic ornament a tortuous corpulence, distorting the proportions of columns, and making monstrous additions to them. But in late sixteenth- and early seventeenth-century England, they supplied modish patterns, which fostered that confusion of ornament with design which so often disfigures the form of Elizabethan and Jacobean furniture, as, over two centuries later, it disfigured Victorian furniture.

Not until the genius of Inigo Jones coaxed order out of that confusion could the English Renaissance be liberated from the ungainly immaturity that deformed the buildings and furniture of its early phase.

When craftsmen inherit a tradition of splendour in design and competence in execution it may injure their inventiveness and render them suspicious of new materials. During the early part of the seventeenth century the men who made furniture in England were oppressed by traditions that were in conflict with their sense of obligation to contemporary European ideas. The things they made were often ugly because of the confusion of thought that had marred the creation of their design. By the decoration of their furniture, the seventeenth-century craftsmen illustrated the changes that were taking place in their civilisation. When any form of culture breaks down or degenerates and is re-placed by a foreign culture, or is followed by a barbaric interlude prior to the re-establishment of a national culture, a tendency to profusion in ornament is often a symptom of the changes to which that particular civilisation is being subjected. The traditional culture of the Middle Ages, the forms, architectural, symbolical and ornamental, of the Gothic craftsmen, were interrupted in the first third of the sixteenth century; and thereafter those who tried to speak in that rich mediaeval language could only stammer. Some craftsmen were still stammering forgotten Gothic words in the seventeenth century, while they tried to master the fluent Italian language of ornament that had intrigued all Europe with its noble cadences for a hundred and fifty years.

The furniture-makers who served wealthy clients came directly under the influence of Court taste in architecture and decoration, that is to say under the influence of Inigo Jones; but the backbone of the furniture-making craft was in the country. In the village workshops chair-makers and cabinet-makers, turners and carvers, were learning to shape and subdue materials and to devise forms that should serve and satisfy the needs of the time. A vast humanising influence was brought to the handling of that hard and beautiful material—oak. English oak is hard to work, even in these days of fine steel and machinery: three hundred years ago with tremendous pains and abundant common sense it was conquered by men who never gave a thought to 'style' or to 'originality' or to 'modernism'. In the England of that day there was no self-conscious searching for something new; but there was untiring research to secure the maximum efficiency in use for the things that were made. Very simple and practical aims governed the ideas of craftsmen, and the ornamenting of the furniture they created was a relief, a personal indulgence, and, quite

9

obviously, at times, a joke that had something of the infectious flavour of Gothic caricature about it. Cultivated Italian or French gentlemen of the period would have laughed at the results as crude, even as the Romans scorned the native Celtic art of the province of Britain twelve hundred years earlier. This sophisticated laughter was provoked by something that had died out in Europe—the common art of the people. All that the Stuart and Cromwellian craftsmen inherited from the tradition of English woodworking and the crafts that served architecture was executive competence. The greatness of Gothic design had gone: its symbolic significance was lost, and as it was unrepresentative of contemporary life it could no longer inspire the making of anything in wood or stone or metal.

There remained a deep understanding of the appropriate enrichment of structural forms. The decoration of furniture became more pleasing as the seventeenth century advanced; concessions made to the Italianate fashions of the early Stuart period were either abolished or greatly modified; and the restraint that denotes sureness of touch and taste distinguished the later Cromwellian and early Restoration work. For a time there was a balanced perfection in this national form of design, this last flowering of the common art of England, and then the lascivious court of Charles II diverted its eyes with foreign fashions, and again the English craftsman had to observe and absorb alien ideas.

It was during the Commonwealth that appreciation for foreign fashions began to grow in a fresh and healthy way. Many keen-eyed, cultivated gentlemen were travelling in those troubled years of England's republican experiment. It was the one safe way of escaping from the variegated discomforts instituted by the intolerance of the Puritan 'Fanaticks'. Mr. John Evelyn, speaking French, Italian and Spanish, familiarised himself with Europe, while at home stern-faced men enforced with barbaric thoroughness the rigours of Puritan idealism. Observant of architecture, appreciative of painting and sculpture, and particularly intrigued by any example of mechanical ingenuity, John Evelyn showed in the pages of his *Diary* how receptive the English mind had become; how ready to absorb and to expand ably in a national idiom the intellectual and artistic stimulus of the Renaissance. What Evelyn was doing as an amateur to improve his taste, architects were also doing as part of their professional training. Studying antique models and admiring them, subjecting their imaginations to the discipline of Vitruvius in the proportions of the things they constructed in stone and wood, the English architects and designers who followed that great and tragic pioneer, Inigo Jones, never allowed their admiration of the antique to entrap them into exact and mindless copying. They understood a system of design, and presently they employed it with copious invention to solve contemporary problems of building. Wren's steeples, like St. Bride's, Fleet Street, or St. Magnus the Martyr in Billingsgate, had no antique prototypes; they were pure inventions, designed in accordance with an ancient system of architectural rhythms. What was done so understandingly in stone in the last third of the seventeenth century was being done in wood by the opening of the eighteenth, and the great age of English furniture had begun.

That the civilised implications of that system of architectural design were comprehended by educated men

in the middle years of the seventeenth century is shown
by an early entry in Evelyn's *Diary* (4th November
1644) when he describes his visit to the Palace Far-
nezi: '. . . a magnificent square structure, built by
Michael Angelo of the 3 orders of columns after the
ancient manner, and when Architecture was but newly
recovered from the Gothic barbarity'. Again, referring
to the great church at Sienna (21st May 1645), he admits with contemptuous surprise that 'the front of this
building, tho' Gothic, is yet very fine'. In such terms
did the English gentleman of the period dismiss the
achievements of mediaeval design. How little succeed-
ing generations respected the first efforts of English
craftsmen to mask the forms evolved by 'Gothic barbarity' with the ornamental mannerisms of the Renaissance is suggested by another passage from Evelyn's
*Diary* (10th November 1644) in which he refers to the
furniture in Prince Ludovisio's villa: 'But what some
look upon as exceeding all the rest, is a very rich bedstead (which sort of grosse furniture the Italians much
glory in, as formerly did our grandfathers in England
in their inlaid wooden ones) inlaid with all sorts of
precious stones and antiq heads, onyxs, achates, and
cornelians, esteem'd to be worth 80 or 90,000 crownes'.

'Gross furniture' certainly describes the over-orna-
mented beds and tables and cupboards that appeared
in the half-century between 1570 and 1620. The Puritan interlude at least helped to rid English furniture of
its vulgar profusion, and when all that Italianate stuff
had been shed, and furniture had been slimmed back to
the bare oak bones of structural needs, it was clear how
strongly Gothic tradition had survived. But this was
the last time it became nationally apparent. Already the

woodworkers in villages all over England were doomed
to the dictatorship of a new order, even as they had been
subjected to the dictatorship of florid disorder by the
Elizabethan new rich.

Furniture-making only illustrated one aspect of the
final struggle for individualism that was made by English craftsmen. Not for individual freedom to 'express'
themselves; but freedom to continue a tradition in which
they worked naturally and happily. They retained some
traces of independence until the restoration of Charles
II. Until 1660 or thereabouts woodworkers had con-
ducted their own affairs, had not been controlled by
particular and precise dictatorship in design, but had
followed, grumblingly no doubt, the ideas of the nobility and gentry. But Charles II and his Court during
their exile acquired more than a superficial regard for
foreign ideas. Like John Evelyn, hundreds of gentlemen expanded their education by travelling in France
and Holland and Italy. They learned to admire all sorts
of new materials and forms.

Walnut began to take the place of oak. Foreign craftsmen, with a mastery of new methods of decoration and
construction, began to settle in London. English craftsmen became even more humble and were reduced to a
position of artistic dependence and servitude. 'Nothing
is more striking than the inability of the English to
stand by their native traditions in art', wrote Professor
G. M. Trevelyan.[1] This is perhaps because the English
are not given to originating great movements in art or
design. They absorb and adapt; but they use their borrowed ideas with such dignity, such restraint and simplicity, that what began as a copy may end as a thing of

---

[1] *England under Queen Anne,* vol. i, chap. iv, p. 87.

great original beauty. There is in England an undying impatience of grandiose ideas and effects.

In 1699 John Pomfret wrote 'The Choice', which summarises in its opening lines the English gentleman's conception of domestic and architectural felicity:

> If Heaven the grateful liberty would give,
> That I might chuse my method how to live,
> And all those hours propitious Fate should lend
> In blissful ease and satisfaction spend:
> Near some fair town I'd have a private seat,
> Built uniform; not little, nor too great;
> Better if on a rising ground it stood,
> On this side fields; on that a neighb'ring wood:
> It should within no other things contain
> But what are useful, necessary, plain:
> Methinks 'tis nauseous, and I'd ne'er endure
> The needless pomp of gaudy furniture.
> A little garden, grateful to the eye,
> And a cool rivulet run murm'ring by,
> On whose delicious banks a stately row
> Of shady limes or sycamores should grow;
> At th' end of which a silent study plac'd,
> Should be with all the noblest authors grac'd.

The English people have always rebelled against palaces. Visions of grandeur have been flashed before them by great architects, but have been rejected or else so modified that little of their ornate impressiveness has been retained. Architects who have behaved in this way have been rapped over the knuckles by their clients and told abruptly to be practical. Sir John Vanbrugh, perhaps the greatest designer of palaces England has ever produced, suffered for his abilities. Blenheim was described by Pope as 'a labour'd quarry above ground', a description that Horace Walpole repeated with relish when criticising with his usual engaging lightness

Vanbrugh's work; but Pope in his much-quoted verses on Blenheim voiced the general distaste for elaboration:

> Thanks, sir, cried I, 'tis very fine,
> But where d'ye sleep, or where d'ye dine?
> I find, by all you have been telling,
> That 'tis a house, but not a dwelling.

Back comes the Englishman to the practical problems of comfort. When architects, furniture-makers and other craftsmen had a sense of fitness and a sense of style, and the educated taste of their patrons encouraged good design, there was a golden age of furnishing which ended in the thirties of the nineteenth century after desire for comfort had debilitated respect for good proportions.

The direction of English craftsmen by professional designers, architects, decorators, artists and modish men of taste—competent or incompetent as the case might be—came in the eighteenth century and persists to the present day. From the oak furniture made between 1640 and 1680, and from its decoration, we may observe the death-bed scenes of mediaeval art in England.

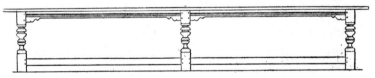

Long table from Penshurst Place, Kent, with turned legs: a late sixteenth-or early seventeenth-century design, unaffected by 'Italianate' ornament. *After Bridgens*. Compare with table on Plate VIII.

## CHAPTER II

# THE HISTORICAL BACKGROUND OF DESIGN
## 1700–1934

EARLY in the eighteenth century the sense of order in design, which had influenced architecture since Inigo Jones had interpreted the spirit of the Renaissance, affected everything that was made in wood, metal or stone. A whole new world of relationships was created. Chairs and tables and coaches, state barges, lanterns, the stern galleries of men-of-war and merchant vessels, door knockers and drawer handles, key plates, fireplaces and chandeliers were all obviously and elegantly related.

In furniture the age of rugged fitness had passed. The chairs, tables and chests of those opening decades of the great century of design no longer illustrated the triumphant skill of the craftsman overpowering tough materials. Mastery of wood was no longer proclaimed by every line of the cabinet-maker's or chair-maker's work. There were impressive advances of skill in decoration. The delicate intricacies of marquetry enriched the surfaces of cabinets, cupboards and bureaux. The veneering of panels was practised, not (as is now often supposed) to provide a cheap way of covering up a cheap and possibly nasty wood with a thin layer of something more elaborate, but to gain the fullest possible decorative value from the beautiful marking of such a wood as walnut. Veneering is a process that can only be carried out by expert craftsmen. It requires time and care and achieves ornamental results that would be impossible if solid panels of wood were used.

The decoration of furniture ceased to be a relaxation for the craftsman, carried out in the spirit of 'Now the job's finished, let's have a bit of fun with it!' The form of the article and its embellishment were conceived in detail before the work was begun. For example, the knees of cabriole legs were sometimes enriched with a carved shell device. This enrichment had to be planned exactly before the leg was made, so that the knee could be given extra thickness to enable the carver to cut back and shape the device. It could never be an afterthought, a 'bit of fun', like some of the chip carving done by Gothic woodworkers. To-day we occasionally find sets of Queen Anne chairs with carving on the knees that has blunted and flattened the subtle, swelling curve of the cabriole form and has made the legs too thin. But this is not the result of a blunder by some early eighteenth-century craftsman; it is usually the work of a modern dealer-cum-faker of antique furniture who has had this spurious ornament carved on an old chair or set of chairs so that he can put up the price after ruining the proportion of the original design.

'Fitness for purpose', that elementary rule of design, was accepted by the craftsmen of the golden age; but it was not allowed to be a controlling influence. In France it was ignored altogether, and although English furniture was affected by French fashions it was always made with a solid regard for use and comfort. Not only were individual articles of furniture conceived in complete detail before they were made, but sets and suites of furniture were designed. All hard lines were softened. Dutch taste, which was so powerful in the late seventeenth century, had introduced soft, swelling curves for the fronts of cupboards and cabinets; the cabriole leg for tables and chairs and cabinet-stands; and the supple intricacies of inlaid decoration for all surfaces.

During the first two decades of the eighteenth century furniture that had simplicity of form and enrichment and elegance of shape was made in England. For comfort and for the delight of the eye it has never been surpassed. Materials have changed. To-day we have tubular steel and canvas, plastics, rubber, patent leather and steel-sprung upholstery, materials and devices transcending the dreams of any Queen Anne or Georgian designer; but no advance has yet been made upon the beautiful proportions or the comfortable shape of the single chairs and elbow chairs and stuffed wing chairs, nor upon the gracious lines of the tables and cupboards and chests and cabinets that were made when Queen Anne still reigned and that great Englishman, Sir Christopher Wren, was still Surveyor-General, and Sir John Vanbrugh, the architect of Blenheim Palace, was Comptroller of the Royal Works.

In early Georgian times furniture passed through a phase of heaviness. The clean simplicity of the Queen Anne work was replaced by a Germanic grossness, chairs and tables and bookcases and cabinets were overloaded with florid carving and gilding. Cabinet work became architectural in its form. A new and exquisite wood was introduced, mahogany, which gradually replaced walnut. That gifted Yorkshireman, Thomas Chippendale, migrated to London, and with his able contemporaries helped to rid furniture design of the coarseness that had thickened its lines. Great architects continued to be born, to be given opportunities to practise, and to make the most of their opportunities. Classic architecture inspired the ideas of all designers. No matter what passing fashions engaged the attention of society, they were harmoniously accommodated by architects and furniture-makers. Sir William Chambers' Chinese studies might impel Chippendale to design things in the 'Chinese Taste', or Horace Walpole's romantic stage scenery at Strawberry Hill might suggest to furniture designers that the 'Gothic Taste' was up-to-date. Whatever they made, they retained their sense of fitness and their sense of proportion until the end of the long Georgian period.

Thomas Sheraton has given his name to a style, and though his sins as a designer are forgotten to-day, his *Drawing Book* and *The Cabinet Dictionary* disclose a fancifulness that was occasionally idiotic, while the ravings of his pencil often anticipated the worst forms of later nineteenth-century taste. Although Sheraton began his career as a journeyman cabinet-maker, he made no furniture. He developed as a designer, and he stuck to his drawing-board, to his teaching of drawing, and to the publication of books of designs, diversifying these activities by preaching and writing tracts. He was never a great fashionable cabinet-maker like Chippendale. His work did not always escape the consequences of ornamental prolixity. He often displayed a delight in ornate forms that must have had a deplorable influence upon those who bought his books of designs.

His earlier work, elegant in its proportion though inclined to flimsiness, was pleasantly decorative. He used satinwood and mahogany and was lavish with delicate inlay and painted decoration. He discarded the cabriole leg and used instead tapering or turned legs for his chairs and sofas. Undisciplined inventiveness marred his later work, and his interpretation of the Greek revival often resulted in rather vulgar complexity. He died in 1806, when that last phase of Georgian taste, the Regency style, had become the English counterpart to the fashions French designers were devising to appease the regal appetites of Napoleon.

The Court of the self-made Emperor with its blaze of uniforms demanded an imposing background. The delicate rhythms of the pre-Republican period were out of tune with ostentatious martial glamour; Louis-Seize designs that were contrived to match a life of carefully cultivated artificiality, when realities were dismissed as tiresome, when it was 'not done' to be practical, and when witty gossip was the most important thing in the world, were not the sort of designs for the power and glory and vulgarity of Napoleon. It was discovered that the virtues of blood and iron could be adequately reflected in gold and mahogany, judiciously cooled by marble, and inventively handled by designers who may have remembered a passing mode for Egyptian ornament that had appeared in the days of Louis XVI, or who may have wished to flatter Napoleon regarding his Egyptian exploits, although one would imagine that the Emperor would have found any reminder of that fiasco unwelcome. But Egyptian ornament was revived, and the domestic furniture of Greece and Rome was reproduced in mahogany and gilded bronze, and reproduced with such faithfulness that examples of furniture from the houses of Pompeii in the Naples Museum recall the atmosphere of Malmaison, a paradoxical situation brought about by the animation with which the Napoleonic designers studied the antique.

When English furniture-makers are influenced by French taste (and this happens about twice a century), they adjust the foreign ideas with considerable skill to the national ideas of comfort. It was not the French Empire style but the Greek revival that affected early nineteenth-century drawing-rooms and dining-rooms in England. For a time the spidery tendencies of the later Sheraton designs were discarded in favour of strong and gracious curves; not the opulent curves of Queen Anne's time, but curves that had a firm continuity in the backs and legs of chairs. The genuflexions of the cabriole were absent: front legs on chairs curved inwards towards the back legs. Formality, restraint and an agreeable understanding of the use of ornament prevailed. Lines of brass inlay gleamed on chair backs and legs, on tables and cabinets. Instead of the load of gilded bronze decoration that comforted Boney and his camp followers, mouldings, masks and paterae, bands and groups of delicate decoration, were carved in wood or composition, and gilded. The fluting of frames and legs were gilded. All this gold flashing in its ruddy mahogany setting gave to the simple lines of the furniture a richness of effect that was never ornate. There was a fashion for rosewood which began well in this period but which degenerated as the Victorian era approached.

The Greek classic revival in furniture design, encouraged by the early nineteenth-century designers, was the last example of the enlightened borrowing of inspiration from antiquity. The influence of this revival, grafted on to the great eighteenth-century tradition of good proportion in design, remained until 1830. It swiftly collapsed after the first third of the nineteenth century, although it was perpetuated here and there in the country by some craftsman who was still spiritually in tune with the Georgian age. Country makers, as usual, were a decade or so behind the modes of the town, and this slowed up the transition from civilised design to absolute barbarism, so that between 1830 and 1850 many well-designed things were made. But the old generation of craftsmen died, and the less attractive pencil prophecies of Sheraton came true, but with a clumsiness that would have horrified Sheraton. Turning was used for the sake of the bulbs and blobs that could be produced for the uglification of chair and table legs. Debased scrollwork sprawled over the arms of chairs, over the backs of sideboards, over mirror frames. All technical ability was dedicated to ornamental effect, and the dissolution of proportion was unobserved, and in the chaos that ensued that basic principle of design, fitness for purpose, was altogether forgotten.

The reason why such gross and ill-proportioned furniture was accepted and even sought after was the complete change in the nature of patronage which had taken place since the close of the eighteenth century. Fashionable makers like Thomas Chippendale, Hepple-white, Shearer, Ince and Mayhew, and many lesser men, were not only designers and craftsmen, or rather direc-tors of craftsmen, but they were also in direct contact with their clients, or if they were not in direct contact with their clients, they were taking their orders from an architect. Both client and architect were educated people. They knew what they wanted, and what they wanted

was something which conformed to the accepted standards of taste; and standards of taste in the eighteenth
century were good. A gentleman knew when a thing
was well or ill proportioned. It was not then considered
rather bad form to display intelligent appreciation for
the design of things, for the shape of a chair or the
section of a moulding.

The gentleman of fashion and the country gentleman
did not represent the whole market for the maker of
furniture. Mr. Chippendale and his kind were not above
fulfilling a commission for a wealthy city merchant. It
was not quite the same thing naturally as being patron-
ised and owed money by extravagant young noblemen,
but it was business, and in those days when mere men of
commerce knew their place, the city merchant was far
too humble to assert his own taste. What was good
enough for my lord was good enough for plain 'Mister',
although the latter might be rolling in wealth from the
profits accruing from the slave trade or some other con-
genial and paying commercial activity. Firms like Chippendale, Haig & Co.[1] were rather like exclusive tailors.
They met the needs of a select clientele, occasionally
permitting new clients to be added. It was not until the
merchant class of customer became the most paying and
the largest that patronage began to undergo the changes
which led to the ultimate ascendancy of wholly uneducated taste. At first the new rich were humble. They
were content to imitate the ideas of the old aristocracy.
They were in that subdued state of ignorance when
'safety first' appears as the only possible slogan for social
salvation. The furniture-makers, also playing for safety,
began to make 'on spec'. They began to make for

---

[1] Chippendale's business was continued under this title until about 1796.

'stock' rather than for individual orders. The individual orders had not ceased. But furniture businesses were growing through the patronage of the commercial class, and to a great extent this new form of trade had to be cultivated with stock. Only as the new rich gained a little more confidence did they outgrow their first innocence, when they had accepted things of good proportion with awe rather than with pleasure, knowing that what pleased a lord must in the nature of things be above suspicion. Their growing confidence made them demand something that *looked* rich. The dignities and noble simplicities of eighteenth-century design no longer satisfied their ideas of affluent comfort.

This was happening nearly everywhere in Europe. England was not the only country dominated by gross and fantastically romantic taste. Orderliness was being forgotten. If we glance at the original illustrations of the *Pickwick Papers*, if we study Seymour's frontispiece, we see Mr. Pickwick dictating in what appears to be, in anticipation of *The Old Curiosity Shop*, a room dismal with Gothic junk, and we get a vivid idea of the failing taste in furnishing, of the increasing tolerance of complication, of the gradual approach of chaos. Even as early as the *Pickwick Papers* the strictures of Dickens on the elaborate process of veneering prove how far the popular mind had drifted from any appreciation of skilled craftsmanship. In the tale told by the bagman, Tom Smart, the hero, addresses an old mahogany chair rather rudely. The chair reproves him, saying: 'That's not the way to address solid Spanish mahogany. Dam'me, you couldn't treat me with less respect if I was veneered.' Again, in *Our Mutual Friend*, Dickens describes Mr. and Mrs. Veneering in a way that suggests they were extremely shoddy and unpleasant people. Through all the confusion, disorder and ignorance which came into the English home during the nineteenth century, the national affection for common sense prevented the rooms from becoming too hopelessly debased, too stupidly remote from realities. There were in this period many eighteenth-century survivals both in furniture and architecture. In one of those early works of moral uplift dedicated to the spiritual elevation of the young, and entitled, *Perambulations in London and its Environs comprehending An Historical Sketch of the Ancient State, and Progress, of the British Metropolis: a Concise Description of its Present State, Notices of Eminent Persons, and a short account of The Surrounding Villages in Letters Designed for Young Persons*, by one Priscilla Wakefield, published during the Regency, there is a description of the London that the Victorians inherited from their educated forefathers:

'If the grandeur of a city is to be determined by the number of magnificent public edifices, Paris must be preferred to London; but if the prize is to be adjudged to the extent of its buildings; the regularity of its streets; the great number of squares; the appearance of industry, comfort, and wealth of its inhabitants;—London obtains the palm. The houses are of a red brick, and built with great uniformity, as to the outward appearance; though they differ much in the number and distribution of the apartments. The kitchens are mostly underground; and the first floor of retail dealers is occupied with the shops, which are arranged and decorated with the greatest neatness and taste. Above these are the rooms for receiving company; and the upper apartments supply the family with bed-chambers. The houses of the great, though generally plain on the outside, afford every convenience and luxury within, that taste, elegance, and art can furnish.'

Priscilla Wakefield even turns the searchlight of her moral scrutiny upon the humbler English householders: 'I believe there is no nation more attentive to domestic comfort than the English; nor more ingenious to contrive every accommodation to render the home-fireside the most agreeable spot in the universe, though it should happen to be in a narrow street, where the light of the sun can scarcely penetrate. This love of home may be attributed to the amiable character and excellent conduct of the females of middle rank, who are in general admirable patterns of conjugal and maternal virtue; devoting their time to the regulation of their families, with a cheerful perseverance, and well-directed attention that endears them to their husbands, without exposing them to the notice of others, which would ill suit their modesty and diffidence, for which they are remarkable.' The 'modesty and diffidence' of those admirable patterns 'of conjugal and maternal virtue' no doubt prevented them from acquiring any semblance of a critical faculty which would have enabled them to exercise some check upon the ideas which makers of furniture presently produced.

The decay of manners which began with the French Revolution, and which was accelerated by the increase of prosperity in Britain, had its effect upon the form of furniture. The easy chair of the mid- and late-nineteenth century would have been regarded not only as an inelegant monstrosity a hundred years earlier, but its shape was such that nobody would have been willing to use it unless they were in a state of complete physical collapse. Until the nineteenth century people sat upright in chairs, and they were content with the very slightest of rakes on the back of winged chairs and Windsor chairs. The habit of sitting upright did not pass without protest. In 1842 Captain Orlando Sabertash published *The Art of Conversation, with remarks on Fashion and Address*. He said: 'There is a practice getting into vogue, almost into a sort of fashion, among young gentlemen who wish to impose upon the unwary, by *nonchalant* airs of affected ease and freedom from restraint, which I must here denounce as a breach of good manners, and a want of all just feelings of propriety;—I mean the practice of lounging in graceless attitudes on sofas and armchairs, even in the presence of ladies. All these vile and distorted postures must be reserved for the library-couch, or arm-chair, and should never be displayed in the society of gentlemen, and still less in that of ladies. In their own houses, ladies must submit to such conduct, as they cannot well leave a visitor to himself: at all other times they should, if they have any respect for their own dignity, give the lounger the cut-direct, and go to some other part of the room. Once denounced, however, as vulgar and uncivil, the nuisance will cease of itself; for the guilty only offend, under the impression of being thought superlatively fine.' If you must lounge you must lounge in private. Unfortunately it did not remain a private habit. It has finally produced the enormous wallows of upholstery which are to-day described as easy chairs and which in a modern room, grouped about the thin red line of an electric radiator, resemble, as Mr. Serge Chermayeff once said, 'a flock of elephants converging upon a glow-worm'.

In the Victorian age furniture designers imagined that three problems existed: (1) the provision of comfort; (2) the provision of useful accommodation; and (3) the provision of ornamental effects. Comfort became associated with upholstered wallows and stuffy fabrics; to provide accommodation various complexities were invented, including the whatnot, the fern-stand, with 'art' pot above and shelves below, and the overmantel with its shelves and cupboards clustering about a mirror. Nothing was exempt from ornament, and no form of ornament was exempt from decorative futility. William Morris, in spite of his romantic mediaevalism and his almost complete dissociation from contemporary life, managed to revive a faint regard for fitness in design, which had a better effect upon the young men who came under his influence than it ever had upon his own passionately decorative work.

By his constant regard for the achievements of the Middle Ages, and by the antiquarian flavour this imparted to all his work and utterances, Morris was unwittingly responsible for the great antique revival that began with the twentieth century. The Victorian age died in the grip of that Continental nightmare, 'New Art'. The violence of that undisciplined fashion prejudiced the Edwardians against anything new at all, so English furnishing passed into a backward-looking phase, in which the past gave up its dead ideas, and the antique dealer was delighted with the nice, kind, credulous world.

A study of the pleasant things people had lived with in the seventeenth and eighteenth centuries did much to encourage, not a sense of design it is true, but awareness of the monstrous clumsiness and ugliness of Victorian work. It also led to the discovery that English furniture of different periods could be associated.

Whether he worked with oak, walnut or mahogany, the English craftsman had always been actuated by a desire to make things comfortable, to give them an air of sturdy worth; and, generation after generation, this gave a family likeness to the things he made. In the early twentieth century there were craftsmen at work who were designing in the true English tradition; not copying old models, like so many craftsmen, who were compelled by popular demand to supplement the supply of genuine antiques. Designers like the late Ernest Gimson and Sidney Barnsley were creating twentieth-century furniture that could stand side by side with mid-seventeenth-century pieces, and be recognisably of the same sound English stock. Gimson and Barnsley perhaps unconsciously drew their inspiration from that period. Their furniture was designed to make the most of the natural attributes of their material: the colour and marking of the woods they used provided sufficient decoration, and they gave subtle emphasis to their designs by varying the surface of doors and panels and drawer fronts.

The Gimson and Barnsley school of design has created one of the two main branches of modern furniture. All the furniture Gimson made (he died in 1919) was intensely individual, but it was also intensely English. It was as English as anything that came out of a Cromwellian, Queen Anne or Georgian workshop. If Charles II had never returned from exile, and the influences that made the Commonwealth had retained their power, it is conceivable that the sort of furniture Gimson was making in the first two decades of our century would have been made in the sixteen-sixties and seventies. It is because of the kinship of Gimson's entirely

29

original designs with the unsullied vigour of pure English taste that found expression between 1640 and 1660 that modern English furniture which owes its existence to his influence is easy to associate with mid-seventeenth-century work and the simpler furniture of Queen Anne's reign.

After the first world war the idea that original furniture design was even remotely akin to 'New Art' died out, though the period styles clung, like old men of the sea, to the taste of the nineteen-twenties. The period styles did not always come back to life with edifying effect: sometimes they were caricatures. Terrible things were done in the names of Chippendale, Hepplewhite and Sheraton; and from the earlier periods of furniture-making, all manner of uncouth monsters were loosed into rooms, simply because the label 'antique' has often been a passport for anything, good, bad, indifferent or indisputably ugly. In no other age has the majority of people preferred to imitate the ideas of a previous age; in no other age have people been fortunate enough to have such an abundance of fresh and agreeable designs from which to choose, designs representing two distinct schools.

The first school of design, based on the work of artist-craftsmen, was as comfortable and familiar as anything we may find in Stuart or Georgian England. Those who followed it, designed furniture on the assumption that houses and rooms will be much the same to-day and to-morrow as they have always been. That sort of modern furniture was part of the English tradition.

The second school was revolutionary, reflecting the revolution that had taken place in architecture, which may change before the end of this century every established conception of house design. The traditional materials for furniture-making were discarded, decorative fabric was slung between chromium-plated steel tubes, creating comfortable but slightly astonishing and rather bleak chairs; sheets of plywood were elevated upon a severely simple steel framework, and the result was a light and not ungracious table. A commodious box of metal-faced plywood was clasped in a frame of steel tubing, and the result was a light and practical sideboard.

Such furniture demanded a setting for itself. It could not at first be associated with the things of tradition. Primarily fit for its purpose, it was restricted to a few basic shapes, for the form of a chair made of steel tubing could not be greatly varied without indulging in needless complexity. This furniture was part of the age of steel, concrete, glass, plastics, light metals and standardisation. While it allowed individual taste to flourish so far as fabrics were concerned, it imposed a ruthless simplicity upon furnishing, so that houses began to interpret the ideal of M. Le Corbusier, who once said, 'The house is a machine for living in'. This idea is wholly abhorrent to English minds, for the English, bereft of frozen Continental logic, have the comfortable belief that a house is a home. (By the nineteen-fifties, functional furniture had become civilised.)

Modern English furnishing can now accommodate this furniture of the structural revolution. The dining-room, essentially a functional apartment where a certain mechanical efficiency is desirable, lends itself particularly to slender things of plated steel or

31

lacquered copper, leather and rubber, plastics and glass. But wood is wood; warm and friendly, it is pleasant to touch and to see. The whole history of English furnishing is a record of discoveries by craftsmen of the pleasant things that could be done with wood—with oak and beech, yewtree, applewood, cherry and elm, and, when fashion insisted, with walnut, mahogany, rosewood and satinwood.

The missionaries and apologists for functional furniture either ignored wood, or dismissed it as an old-fashioned, obsolete material. But wood has a tremendous advantage which hard, bright, industrially produced materials lack: it improves with age and mellows in colour year by year, unless it has been stupidly spoiled by some stain put on to create the illusion of an 'antique finish'.

While the work of such twentieth-century furniture designers as Sir Ambrose Heal, Sir Gordon Russell, Ernest Gimson and Sidney Barnsley keeps alive much that is best in English furniture, while their designs may appear side by side with the oak, walnut and mahogany furniture of the past, the furniture of the structural revolution had at first to sit by itself. It was later designed in a manner that allowed it to be used with other types of furniture.

Early in the nineteen-thirties, furniture by that talented Finnish architect, Alva Aalto, illustrated a new humanised technique for the manipulation of plywood. His work, which was exhibited in London during the autumn of 1933, strongly influenced English designers in the use of this decorative and malleable material.[1]

[1] Illustrations of this furniture were published in the *Architectural Review*, vol. lxxiv, No. 445, December 1933, pp. 220-21.

There is, of course, spurious modernism in furniture, even as there are spurious antiques. The 1925 Paris Exhibition of Decorative Art released an epidemic of florid ornament in this country, and upon chairs, beds, cabinets and other articles there was an outbreak of fruit and flowers and a profusion of mixed vegetation, all rendered in a flat, conventional way, and frequently enlivened with inappropriate colour. One good thing came to England from that Exhibition, and that was a reawakened interest in the decorative beauty of wood surfaces. Amboyna, figured walnut and some of the Empire woods came into favour, and to give the utmost value to their natural ornamental qualities, carved enrichment was restricted.

Most periods have produced not only distinctive styles, but some distinctive pieces of furniture related to some new invention in comfort or manners or entertainment. Our opportunity has been the gramophone and the radio and television cabinet. At first disguise was the chief aim of manufacturers, but some had the wit to employ designers of the standing of Wells Coates, Gordon Russell and R. D. Russell.

Few periods have been richer in potential influences for distinguished design than our own; few periods have mishandled their opportunities with such repellent fertility. We are now emerging from the phase of nervous dependence upon tradition. As a result of that phase, cheap imitations of the most showy objects of the eighteenth-century squire's drawing-room are still crammed into the parlours of semi-detached England, where they gradually disintegrate as the final instalments for their purchase become due. But although we are saying good-bye to all that, we have only exchanged

4

tyrants. Tradition has been dethroned, but the dictatorship of the *New Materials* has for a time tended to repress
any little individual freedoms designers might have
hoped to indulge. As we have seen, sympathetic understanding of the nature and limitations of material has in
the past endowed English furniture design with agreeable character; but now we are in danger of exchanging
that discerning mastery of materials for spineless servitude. Even 'fitness for purpose', which began as a piece
of good, basic common sense, is sometimes used as a
liturgical formula, which is chanted when ever imagination is exorcised from design.

Most of the inspiration in furniture design comes
from outside the industry. From those independent
research workers in design, the artist-craftsmen, and
frequently from architects—the only class in the whole
community trained in design, and trained to think
logically and lucidly about materials. There are a few
firms in the furniture trade, controlled by men with
good taste who understand how to employ designers or
who are themselves designers.

To-day we have these broad classifications of furniture design: the rustic school, or wood, dear wood,
naked and unashamed. The mechanistic school,
softened by a few concessions to coarse, commonplace ideas of comfort. Finally, furniture designed by
people who use imagination and not creeds for the
shaping of their designs. It is possible to choose contemporary designs that can make a twentieth-century
domestic interior as tranquil in form and colour and as
satisfying in visual and bodily comfort as any home in
any other period of the history of English furniture-
making.

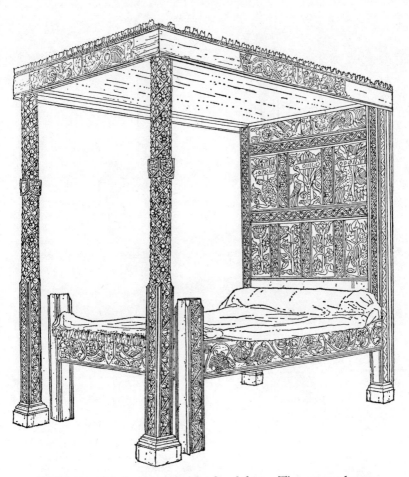

English posted bed, with carved head and frame. The octagonal posts
supporting the tester are separated from the frame. *Circa* 1530. The
original example is in the Victoria and Albert Museum. Drawn by
Maureen Stafford, and reproduced from *Guide to Furniture Styles:
English and French* (A. & C. Black Ltd.).

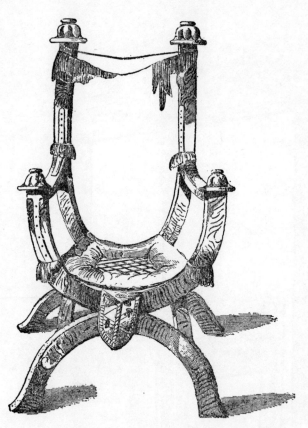

*Above*: Fɪɢ. 1. Chair with X-shaped frame originally covered with fabric and leather, and preserved in the vestry of York Minster. From Henry Shaw's *Specimens of Ancient Furniture* (1836). Chairs of this type, constructed by coffer-makers, date back to the fifteenth century.

*Left*: Fɪɢ. 2. An early seventeenth-century coffer-maker's chair, with a cushioned seat.

## CHAPTER III

## FURNITURE DESIGN UNDER THE WOOD-WORKERS, 1500–1660

CRAFTSMEN have nearly always worked under control. The picture of the craftsman wandering about the country carving this, that and the other object in wood and stone and splashing colour about with splendid freedom dates from the William Morris period. Since then the legend has been elaborated, not without the assistance of Messrs. Chesterton and Belloc, until the Middle Ages has become a gaudy confusion of craftsmen singing continuously, performing feats of pious artistry upon stonework, perched high up on the scaffolding of a new cathedral, or carving joyously (no mediaeval carver ever carved except joyously) some simple thing in oak, something worthy, something honest, something strong and everlasting. It is a pretty picture, but it should be described frankly as a vision instead of an authentic portrait of the Middle Ages. Actually the work of the mediaeval craftsmen was rigidly controlled. It was not a casual activity nor a mystic, emotional calling, although the ornamental side of it must often have been recreation, and, judging by the amount of incomplete ornamental work, recreation that was often interrupted and seldom resumed.

A man could not be a craftsman until he had survived the rigours of a long and severe training, nor was he allowed to practise and use good material unless those responsible for his training were satisfied with his ability. This system of training, controlled by the Guilds, prevented the direction of work from getting into incompetent hands. People who were mediocre in talent, although hard-working, did the less showy jobs. They made the unimportant things without having many opportunities for ornamenting their work.

The earliest form of furniture which craftsmen were required to produce was the chest. The chest has a most respectable ancestry, going back to Greek and early Egyptian times.[1] In England it was the first receptacle, and it was also a seat. It was sturdy, fit for its purpose, and often unbeautiful in spite of the generally applicable formula that Norman Douglas expresses in the happy phrase: 'There is a beauty in fitness no art can enhance'. In the fifteenth and early sixteenth centuries it was still the principal article of furniture in English houses, and the chests and coffers of those days have been grossly parodied and multiplied in our own time by the fakers of old England. The chest form has also inspired some of the regrettable creations of what may be called 'Garden Suburb Art'. There is nothing to admire in the crude strength of primitive furniture-making, but too often our own stimulating century is represented by inept imitations of pre-Tudor work, and the possibilities of contemporary materials are ignored.

The earliest English chests were just boxes with hinged lids. Inside when you opened the chest there was a little ledge or shelf just under the lid at the side. This ledge or shelf is found in the earliest chests that

[1] The Egyptian mummy-case was a long chest.

have survived.[1] We think, perhaps rightly, of the mediaeval house as a place haunted by strong and evil smells. Habits in the castle were as casual and insanitary as they were in the serf's hovel. But smells of an agreeable delicacy were appreciated, perhaps far more than they are to-day when we have exchanged the smell of stagnant sewage for the fumes of petrol. The ledge in early English chests was put there to accommodate lavender or some other sweet herb, perhaps dried woodruff, so that the contents would be fragrant. Sometimes this ledge is mistakenly described as a place where money was kept. While some chests had secret receptacles for valuables, it is obvious that an open ledge in the most get-at-able place immediately below the lid would not be used for storing them.

The terms 'chest' and 'coffer' are, according to some writers, interchangeable.[2] *Cofre* is the archaic French equivalent, *coffre-fort* meaning a safe. In German and Dutch the word *koffer* means a box or chest or travelling trunk, the Scandinavian variants being: *koffert* (Swedish) and *kuffert* (Norwegian and Danish). Originally the word was derived from the Greek name for basket. Its connection with a receptacle is ancient, and this is important because *coffering* is an architectural term for the repetition of square sunk panels in a ceiling.[3] It is, perhaps, reasonable to assume that the coffering method of ceiling construction should have derived its name from

[1] A thirteenth-century chest formerly in the collection of the late Mr. Robert Atkinson has one of these ledges. See Plate I.

[2] Herbert Cescinsky begins chapter i of volume ii of *Early English Furniture and Woodwork* with the words: 'The chest or coffer was a most important article of furniture. . . .'

[3] 'Coffer, a deep panel in a ceiling' (J. H. Parker's *Concise Glossary of Terms used in Grecian, Roman, Italian and Gothic Architecture*).

chests which are panelled. The most primitive form of chest is a large block of wood, hollowed out. Early chests are slabbed, not panelled, the fronts, backs and sides each being made from single pieces of wood, joined and pegged. Chests were usually solid and substantial pieces of furniture, whereas a coffer, in mediaeval England, was a portable receptacle, the equivalent of a trunk, which could be packed with clothes and valuables. It was generally a wooden box, covered with leather, and was the work of a coffer-maker or cofferer, who was a leather worker. The coffer was also a strong box, a form of timber safe for storing treasure. Chaucer uses it in this sense in *The Legend of Good Women* (the later version, lines 380-81):

> And is his tresour, and his gold in cofre,
> This is the sentence of the philosophre.

Chaucer also calls an elm coffin a cofre (*The Parlement of Foules*, line 177).

The cassone was an Italian elaboration of the chest, a shapely and ornate receptacle that was never made in England. Until the end of the fourteenth century English chests were of the simplest kind, occasionally embellished with a little chip carving—geometric roundels that had about them something faintly Saracenic, as if some fluttering and feeble echo of the taste of returning crusaders had been caught and perpetuated by the carver.

Only when carved ornamentation grew bolder did its affinities with contemporary Gothic work become so pronounced that the front of a late fifteenth- or early sixteenth-century chest often resembled a series of blind church windows; tracery with the voids narrowed and reduced, masking the surface. This carved tracery would be pierced in the panelled door of an aumbry, to provide ventilation, for the aumbry (which is sometimes called an ambry) was a mediaeval food cupboard. Originally it was a recess formed in the thickness of a wall and enclosed by wooden doors; and from this a free standing cupboard evolved. A wall aumbry in a church, near the altar, was used for sacramental vessels, and was known as an almery. The aumbry and the press were the earliest forms of enclosed cupboard.

The function of receptacles sometimes influenced the form of ornament that was carved upon them. The linen-fold device was an attempt to illustrate the folded fabrics within the chest or cupboard. The resulting pattern was so pleasing in its form, so subtle in the surface variation it afforded, that it was adopted for the embellishment not only of the fronts of chests and cupboards, but for the walls of rooms whenever they were panelled. The vine leaf motif, flowing and boldly decorative, was occasionally used, but in spite of such experiments with independent ornamental forms, the embellishment of early Tudor furniture never wholly lost its affinity with church woodwork.

During the sixteenth century, chests and stools which had hitherto provided the seats in most dwellings were supplemented by chairs. There had been chairs before this time, but they were in the nature of state chairs, rare and lordly things that seldom strained beneath the weight of a commoner. Generally these chairs were squat, throne-like boxes with rigid arms and high, straight backs. They were chairs that looked as though they had been designed to carry enormous weights. The enclosed front below the seat, the solid sides and the vertical back were usually filled with ornamental lines of tracery carved upon the panelled oak. At the upper corners of the back there would be finials, carved like spires (as in the Coronation Chair at Westminster Abbey), or else terminating in little castellated platforms to accommodate selections from the fauna of heraldry. The X-shaped chair consisting of a wood frame with a fabric seat and back represented the same principle of construction as some of the modern chairs made of tubular steel.[1] There is a fourteenth- or fifteenth-century X-shaped chair in the vestry of York Minster. (See page 36.) Even in Tudor days these chairs were rare. They might be found in the palace of a nobleman or some rich ecclesiastic. In the early sixteenth century they were the elegant and comfortable representatives of the Italianate fashions that were soon to invade England. They no more represented the contemporary English craftsman's idea of chair-making than the classic façade of some composition by Baldassare Peruzzi or Giacomo Barozzi represented an English mason's idea of church-building.

The years of conflict that England suffered during the sixteenth century were illustrated by the troubled hesitancies of the ornament used for enriching furniture. In the opening and middle years of that century two forms of civilisation were meeting but not merging. The old social order was deliberately broken up by the rulers of the state. Everything associated with mediaeval civilisation was lost or distorted. The problems in furniture design that were beginning to be explored by Gothic craftsmen were neglected or else loaded with alien and un-English mannerisms.

[1] See Fig. 2, p. 36.

The chair was still left in a clumsy state of development. It was still only a box turned into a throne, an unfriendly shape. Even when the box disappeared and the chair became a stool with a back, its hard seat elevated upon legs, its deficiencies were those of its mediaeval progenitor. Although chairs in the sixteenth century were not so rare as in previous ages, they were uniformly uncomfortable, excepting only the luxuriant X-shaped models.

The ubiquitous chest which served as a seat and occasionally as a table, was by the middle of the Tudor century being restricted to its original use in well-appointed houses. Chairs (uncomfortable, but still chairs) and what were called buffet stools were becoming common. The latter were probably joined stools. The free standing cupboard or press, and the court cupboard were giving accommodation. Tables which began as crude benches on a large scale acquired some structural refinements. They were mostly of the trestle type, with a strong leg at either end, firmly set into a wide base and connected by horizontal members called stretchers. These two legs upheld bracketed cross-pieces on which the board rested. They were simple in design and very strong. (Fig. 7, page 45.) They were presently replaced by the four-legged table. Extra legs were added as the length increased, so that by the end of the sixteenth century six- and eight-legged tables were being made.

Beds had before the sixteenth century been designed upon the principle of making a room within a room. This principle controlled bed design until the nineteenth century. (The awful experience of Mr. Pickwick in the wrong double bedroom at the Great White Horse at Ipswich could only have occurred in an age of completely enclosed beds.) With their heavy framework and their concealing curtains such beds were separate sleeping chambers constructed of wood and fabric. The tester, or roof of the bed, was of panelled wood, so was the back, and the tester was supported in front by two posts. The curtains hung from the tester. All this woodwork provided an area for carving, and it overflowed with ornament as, year by year, the sparkling ripples of Italian fashion eroded English ideas of decoration. (See illustration on page 35.)

In architecture and in furniture design, the opening years of the sixteenth century had promised a vigorous national style. Hampton Court showed how orderly and comfortable that style was. It was lost in the age of confusion that for nearly one hundred years loaded furniture design with vulgar and coarse decoration, and destroyed the simplicity of form and the dignity that were beginning to emerge from the strength and solidity of mediaeval woodworking.

Between 1580 and 1630 English furniture included chests, press cupboards, court cupboards, turned chairs and joint (or joined) stools, and tables with turned legs. There were armless chairs with upholstered seats and backs, the so-called farthingale chair of the early seventeenth century, to accommodate ladies who wore that expansive garment, and the contemporary name was back stool—a stool with a back. There were beds like nightmare Roman temples, with the posts supporting the tester consisting of columns broken by melon bulbs, hideously proportioned, in every way as vulgar as the worst efforts of mid-Victorian furniture makers. All this furniture suffered from ornament that was copied from

Fig. 3. Early XVIth-century chest with linen-fold panels.
Figs. 4, 5. Chair and low standing cupboard of the same period.
Fig. 6. Early XVIIth-century chest in oak.
Fig. 7. Early XVIth-century trestle table.
Figs. 8, 9. Mid-XVIIth-century chest with drawers, and table.
Fig. 10. Early XVIIth-century oak side table.

books. It was intended to look rich. It succeeded in looking fidgety.

The whole Elizabethan scene is rather overcharged with new and exciting and ill-digested ideas. Only in literature, in dramatic art and in music were clarity, order and greatness achieved. In literature it was an age of stupendous achievement—the poets and dramatists overshadowed every other kind of creative artist. For their works posterity has reverence. But if we examine with critical eyes the decoration and architecture and the shape of furniture produced at that time; if we put away the thought that such things formed the setting for those wild and splendid gentlemen who did such magnificent things for the sake of English trade overseas, whose manners were so exquisite and whose accomplishments were so strikingly various; if we forget about the virile and stimulating life that was lived against this clumsy background and look only at the constituents of the background, then we must condemn them as unwieldy and monstrously ugly. There were a few examples of agreeably decorated furniture. There was some fine, clean carving. But such lucid exceptions only occurred when craftsmen were not harnessed to the imported fashions of the Continent.

All the pieces of furniture that had come into use by the end of the sixteenth century developed and changed during the seventeenth century. Cupboards were used more extensively. The terms press-cupboard and court-cupboard should be defined. The press-cupboard was a tall piece of furniture with a big cupboard in the lower part of it and in the upper part smaller cupboards, set back with a ledge in front. The top of this smaller set projected like a roof, and was supported by two turned columns, often of the melon bulb pattern. (Fig. 11, page 49, also Plate VII.) The court-cupboard consisted of two open shelves, supported by columns in front and by columns or flat vertical members behind with a pot board at the base. This type of court cupboard is sometimes called a buffet. Some have a small central cupboard in the upper part. (Fig. 13, page 49, also Plate VI.)

The chest was continuing its evolution, and early in the seventeenth century a new species was created. The base of the chest grew deeper, and in that base a couple of drawers were fitted and the result was called a mule chest. That was the beginning of the chest's gradual elevation from seat level to higher altitudes, which culminated in the eighteenth-century tallboy or double chest. Later in the seventeenth century, chests staggered up on to stands, variously proportioned and often mere excuses for decoration. The combination of the chest and cupboard was more satisfying to the utilitarian instincts of the English, and this form of chest was made in the Puritan period, when arid utility engaged the minds of the pious hooligans who were busy eliminating comfort, innocent amusements, Christmas customs, Charles I, and anything else that happened to be ornamental.

During the first forty years of the seventeenth century there was no modification in the bald discomfort of chairs. Leather seats and backs were introduced during the Commonwealth, but no improvement was made in the general shape of the chair which might have increased its agreeableness. The X-shaped types were perpetuated and they developed rich depths of comfort, becoming broader, with deeply cushioned seats, and with the wooden frame covered completely with fabric. Tasselled fringes hung down from the seat and arms; the fabric on the framework was garnished with gilded nails; but such chairs were still rare. An example of this type, preserved until a few years ago in the Cottage Hospital at Moreton-in-the-Marsh, is now in the Victoria and Albert Museum. It resembles the chair used by Charles I during his trial, and there are similar chairs at Knole. (See Fig. 2, page 36.) It is a coffer-maker's chair, and is structurally the same as the fifteenth-century example of that craftsman's work in the vestry of York Minster, only the seat and back are more rigid and are not slung from the frame. This chair suggests the conscious preservation of a structural form for the sake of decorative effect because its rigid seat and back make no use of the structural bones of the chair. The X-shaped framing below is without significance in this early Stuart example. It could just as well have four independent legs. It represents the last phase of the X-shape type in England until we come to certain modern steel types in which the X-shaped framing again fulfils a structural need.

Chairs that derived their decoration from elaborate upholstery, from rich fabrics and braiding and intricately knotted fringes, were swept away some years before Charles I—himself a survival from a luxurious period—was compelled to sit in one of the type just described during his trial. The Puritans repressed luxury, and insisted upon plainness and stern statements of utility. Velvets, fine silks and brocades, elaborate carving and inlaid ornament, and all the foreign tricks that had been lifted from the plates of the Continental copy books, were banished. Of all the misplaced

48

FIG. 11. Oak press-cupboard, c. 1620.

FIG. 12. Oak bed, late XVIth century.

FIG. 13. Oak court-cupboard, late XVIth or early XVIIth century.

FIG. 14. Oak table, c. 1630–40.

FIG. 15. Oak chair, with inlaid panels in the back and carved cresting, c. 1600.  FIG. 16. Oak joint stool, c. 1570.

FIGS. 17, 18. Early XVIIth-century stool covered in velvet, and back stool—or so-called farthingale chair.

5

architectural *motifs* that had helped to destroy good proportion in furniture, only the arcaded panel remained. Arcading was a form of ornament which reproduced arches in flat relief, singly or in series, on panels and friezes, the upper part of each panel being filled by an arch springing from crudely fluted pilasters. All the other architectural loans to furniture making were repudiated. No longer did Ionic and Doric columns masquerade with dropsical emphasis as table-legs and bed-posts. There was a revival of the type of ornament that was derived naturally from the skill of the woodworker and the turner. Running patterns and ornamental patches were punched into the surface of wood. There was a great increase of ability in turning. The legs of chairs and tables were turned in baluster forms, and presently decorative turnings were evolved, such as a succession of bobbins, and, in time, the highly ornamental barley sugar twist. A significant and perhaps unfortunate development took place during this period of comparative abstention from ornament, and it grew out of the increased facility for decorative turning. Balusters and strips of bobbin turning were split centrally, and the flat side applied to a surface—generally to the framework of a chest or to a panel.[1] Hitherto ornament had been worked by a carver on some solid, structural member of the piece of furniture. Panel mouldings were 'struck' and worked on the edges of the styles and rails of the framework.

Even in the late sixteenth century, inlaid marquetry was used for friezes and panels, such woods as holly and sycamore being inserted in an oak ground. It was rather crude work, and did not attain higher standards

[1] Split turning in stone was used in the late sixteenth century.

of workmanship until at least a century later. (Some elaborate chests, with inlaid representations of the Palace of Nonesuch, were occasionally found in England in the late sixteenth century, but it is unlikely that they were of English workmanship; they have a Flemish flavour about them.)

Applied ornament was a new practice, and although it was used with restraint in the mid-seventeenth century, it was the precedent for many infelicitous experiments which disfigured the work of later periods and which reached the zenith of ineptitude in pre-war machine-made Jacobean furniture, or 'Jaco' as it is called in the furniture trade. At the end of the early Stuart period when Court taste was ceasing to influence design, the Englishman's house was beginning to be very comfortable. It was not overcrowded; it was light, with tall windows ascending to the ceilings of the rooms; it was probably draughty and rather cold, but it had chairs and tables and cupboards, chests, comfortable beds and decorative textiles on some of the walls. The chairs were becoming more humanised in shape although they were still rigid. Hard, wooden seats were generally used for chairs, stools and settles. There would probably be more stools than chairs in any house, the 'joyned' stool or joint stool being a common article of furniture. These little stools were strong and well-made: it was necessary, for their framing was occasionally subjected to violent tests, particularly in inns when they were flung about during drunken brawls. All this furniture was made of oak. It had to stand wear and tear of a kind unknown in periods that are less virile in character. Those heavy topped oak tables, the long boards supported on six bulbous legs, were framed, braced and wrought to cope with orgies, thunderous expressions of good-fellowship and clamorous outbursts of disapproval. Only the strongest furniture could have survived such vehement social customs.

Oak was no longer tortured into fanciful shapes after the Puritans really began to control England. Released from the necessity of mastering forms that were still unfamiliar in spite of the alluring pictorial directions in works on classic ornament and architecture, the English craftsmen became inventive. New forms of furniture arrived. There was the gate-legged table: a most ingenious mechanical device of extreme simplicity and foreshadowing many latter-day solutions of the economical use of space. The mule chest has already been described, but that was the forerunner of the tallboy which in the eighteenth century was to provide double the accommodation of an ordinary chest without making any extra demand upon floor area. Economies of space and the convenient disposition of furniture in rooms were matters that received a lot of inventive attention everywhere in the seventeenth century.[1] Dual-purpose furniture was also made, notably the table-chair, which was an arm-chair with a circular back, this back being hinged so that it could swing over and assume a horizontal position on the arms, becoming thereby a small circular table. In his travels John Evelyn was meeting various pieces of foreign ingenuity in furniture-making. He speaks of '. . . a chayre to sleepe in with the leggs stretcht out' which can 'draw out longer or shorter'

[1] Oliver P. Bernard has described (in the *Architectural Review*, vol. lxxii, No. 433, December 1932, pp. 285-7) a one-roomed flat of 1684, designed by Cornelius Meyer, a Dutch engineer, who included this and other examples of his ingenuity in a volume entitled *L'arte di restituire Roma: la tralasciata navigazione del suo Tevere,* which he dedicated to Pope Innocent XI.

(10th November 1644). Also '. . . a whimsical chayre, which folded into so many varieties as to turn into a bed, a bolster, a table, or a couch' (29th November 1644).

The pre-Renaissance tradition in woodwork was now fairly re-established. It kept its hold on the country for a long time. It was that tradition, surviving in village workshops, which was responsible—even in the eighteenth century—for the invention of simple 'functional' types of furniture, such as the Windsor Chair, types which only faintly reflected the ideas and forms that were ruling the centres of contemporary fashion.

Even during the Commonwealth, the background of furniture was changing. It was becoming more orderly, losing its congestions of ornament, disclosing in every line and detail the increasing knowledge of architectural proportion, the increasing respect paid by architects to Vitruvian rules. Inigo Jones, that great and tragic father of English architecture, had by the lucidity of his own interpretation of classic architecture abolished the discords that had made the houses and rooms of the early seventeenth century so restless, so pretentiously trivial. Had he lived in a happier period he might have anticipated the direction of furniture design by the architectural profession that came about in the eighteenth century. In his day he was a modernist: though even with the backing of royal patronage he had to endure the futile criticism of the architecturally uneducated, the opposition of the common mind, and the abuse of jealous and stupid people who feared what they could not understand. His historic quarrel with Ben Jonson arose from Jonson's inability to see that Jones was more than a sort of superior scene-shifter for the court masques, and in that prolonged and bitter difference Ben Jonson, genius though he was, proved that he was before all other things a narrow professional literary man. When Jones gathered up all the tangled odds and ends of Italianate fashions, and with profound scholarship and noble imagination wove the most majestic forms, when he disclosed to a world that was fumbling architecturally the lucid harmonies of the Banqueting Hall, that tiny section of the great Palace of Whitehall that was never completed, he roused and shocked, stimulated and exalted the ideas of that world. His later professional life was spent fighting for good design against the dread English Trinity: Ignorance, Indolence and Individualism. No good architect has since been absolved from that unending warfare.

The grandeur of proportion that followed the new understanding of architecture in the middle years of the seventeenth century was matched by the dignity of oak furniture to which national character was restored. Every piece of that furniture was a downright statement of structural fact. It was plain English, with here and there a jest, a light touch of relaxation, the irrepressible humour of the race that had its lively way with wood under a humourless regime, as blithely as it has had its way in most other matters ever since. Those touches of ornament on chair-backs and table-legs might have shown the Puritan governors of the land how impossible it was to drive from English minds a love of enjoyment and a warm regard for the small and pleasant things of the world; how impossible it was to concentrate the thoughts of every subject in that queer repressive English republic upon the rewards of a glum Nonconformist paradise. Soldiers and saints made an art-proof combination. Men of education and alert intelligence gave up

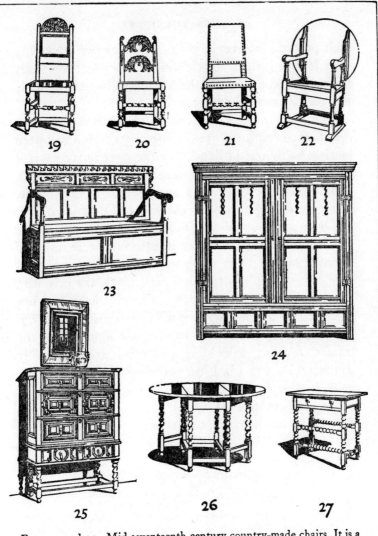

FIGS. 19 and 20. Mid-seventeenth-century country-made chairs. It is a modern habit to apply regional names to these chairs, such as Derbyshire, Yorkshire and Lancashire.

FIG. 21. Leather-covered oak chair, c. 1650.

FIG. 22. Oak table-chair, c. 1655.

FIGS. 23, 24. Oak settle and press, c. 1650.

FIG. 25. Walnut mirror, c. 1680, and oak chest with drawers.

FIGS. 26, 27. Oak gate-leg table and table with bobbin-turned legs and stretchers, c. 1660.

their partisan interest in politics and religion; devoting their leisure instead to scientific enquiry and the study of the arts, consoled by the hope that Puritan tyranny was only a passing madness.

The Puritans had a sobering and clarifying effect on the character of furniture. Before 1630 design had been getting badly out of hand. For the next thirty years it shed all manner of shoddy accumulations of ornament, and by the time Charles II was restored to the throne, furniture was again wholly national and functional, as it had been at the opening of the sixteenth century, before the foreign influences of the Renaissance were imposed upon it; but by 1660 there was a far greater variety of furniture, and in chair design particularly the inventive advance had been enormous. Chairs were now upholstered in leather, with stuffed seats and backs (fig. 21, page 55); sometimes leather was slung from the frames, forming a yielding and most unpuritanically comfortable seat. English woodworkers, having regained control over the form of furniture, were now ready to be influenced by a fresh set of foreign ideas. Charles II did not disappoint them.

Fig. 28. Arcaded panels were used on chests, bed-heads, press cupboards and chimney-pieces from the late sixteenth century to the end of the seventeenth. (See Fig. 12, page 49, also Plates IV and VII.)

## CHAPTER IV

# FURNITURE DESIGN UNDER FASHION
## 1660–1730

MUCH could be written about the influence of courtesans upon furniture design. The phases of elaboration in furnishing that have generally followed the domination of a European king by a mistress or series of mistresses, might suggest that ostentation is symptomatic of moral laxity; but actually there may be an economic explanation of the phenomenon. 'Put not your trust in Princes' favours' has been one of the guiding precepts of beautiful, accomplished and unprincipled women who have studied the exploitation of a monarch, while 'get what you can while the getting is good' is a policy that naturally arises from a realistic consideration of the transitory nature of royal affections. Everything, therefore, that could bear costly and expensive decoration upon its surface was demanded by the uncrowned queens of Europe. Cabinets inlaid and embossed with silver and gold. Exquisite carving, heavily gilded. Plate. Jewels of course. Rich fabrics. Everything that sparkled and glittered and was loaded down with the evidence of wealth appealed to the taste of people who were collecting precious material as fast as they could, material which could easily be turned into money; gauds that would also impress the whole world with the fact that His Gracious Majesty was really taking the most energetic delight in honouring the recipient.[1]

Charles II encouraged many foreign fashions both in furniture design and in ornament. His mistresses encouraged elaboration. Within twenty years of the Restoration, the clean, austere furniture forms that emerged during the Puritan period had disappeared from the fashionable town houses. They survived in the country. But in London new forms multiplied and they were embellished with everything that could symbolise the lascivious preoccupations of Court taste. It was in such malleable branches of design as furniture-making that Carolean ideas found their most luxurious expression.

In architecture a fine orderliness was emerging and Inigo Jones's successor, Sir Christopher Wren, was completing the education of the English in architectural design. It was not until the beginning of the eighteenth century that the form of furniture began to reflect in wood the nobility that was being achieved in stone. Before that harmony was attained there was a florid interval during which furniture was made which had something of the stiffness of line, something of the sturdy uprightness that were common in Puritan times. But those stern, staunch frames were bedecked in a manner which created a strange unseemliness of

---

[1] See Evelyn's description of the dressing-room of the Duchess of Portsmouth (4th October 1683): 'Then for Japan cabinets, screens, pendule clocks, greate vases of wrought plate, tables, stands, chimney furniture, sconces, branches, braseras, &c. all of massive silver, and out of number. . . .' But Charles did not stop at gifts of expensive furniture. He granted the famous palace of Nonesuch to George, Lord Grandison, and Henry Brouncker in trust for Barbara Palmer, Duchess of Cleveland, who, of course, had it pulled down.

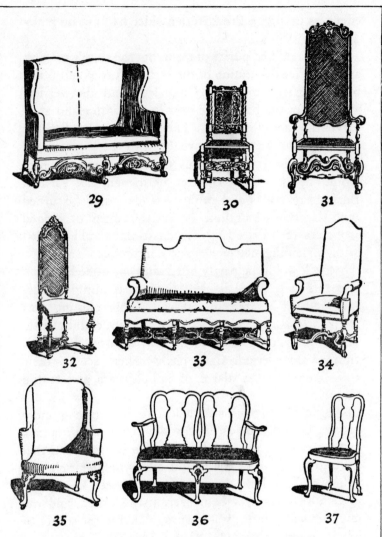

FIG. 29. Settee with walnut frame covered in velvet, c. 1685–90.
FIG. 30. Walnut single chair with cane seat, c. 1670.
FIGS. 31, 32, 33, 34. Walnut chairs and settee, c. 1690.
FIG. 35. Walnut easy-chair covered in needlework, early XVIIIth century.
FIGS. 36, 37. Walnut settee and chair, c. 1710.

59

effect, as though a Presbyterian elder had put on fancy dress.

Chairs retained purity of form, but the simple turning and tentative decoration of the sixteen-forties and fifties became more emphatic. Chair-legs and the vertical members of the back were now linked with elaborately carved horizontal framing. The stretchers that tied the legs together were either twisted with the barley-sugar twist or carved with various decorative *motifs*. These would be carved by country craftsmen, not turned: the legs of tables and cabinet-stands would be turned with bobbin decoration or in the form of ringed balusters. (See Plate IX.) The chair-seat would be filled with a yielding net of elegantly interlaced cane-work. The back would be partly filled with the same material, and this cane panel flanked by carved uprights, surmounted by a crested top rail. This cresting was frequently adorned by the voluptuously chubby little cupids that fluttered about in pairs all over the furniture of this period. Cane chair-makers set up their own shops, to the alarm of upholsterers and textile manufacturers.

Single chairs and armchairs were becoming more ornate. Oak was discarded by the fashionable makers, and walnut was used, a sleek, golden brown wood that gave to the form of chairs and tables greater riches of colour and marking than had hitherto been known.

Comfort was now being seriously studied, and the apparatus of comfort was always related to the source of heat in rooms. Visible heat has guided all English ideas of comfort, so that they are now, even in this age of central heating and electricity, still focussed upon the fireplace. The business of conserving the heat of a fireside and providing protection from draughts has been taken very seriously by every maker of furniture in England. When the literature of the eighteenth and nineteenth centuries refers to the comfort of homes and inns, the chimney-corner, the fireside circle, and the generous depth of inn kitchen fireplaces, flanked by settles, are described in affectionate detail. The high-backed settle was probably the earliest attempt to secure for those who were warming their feet by the fire some guarantee of immunity from partial freezing; for draughts have apparently always plagued the English house, and chill winds have whistled under doors and through window-frames for centuries. The high-backed settle was a severe seat, uncushioned, though acknowledging the existence of the human form in the gentle rake of the back, which rose high above the heads of those leaning against it. (The seats in the third-class compartments of old-fashioned railways preserved the primitive features of the early settle in their archaic purity.) The flanking settles of a sixteenth- or seventeenth-century inn or parlour fireplace extended like wings, concentrating the heat, and their ends were partially enclosed by shaped draught-excluders. It was this form of ear-protecting device that was adopted by the seventeenth- and eighteenth-century furniture-makers for that triumph of comfort, the easy-chair with wings or lugs. It was sometimes called a lug chair; the term wing chair is modern, and it has been called a 'grandfather' chair only since about 1880. Hepplewhite calls an easy chair a saddle cheek.

This progenitor of the easy-chair was suited to the English temperament. It gave a touch of individual isolation even in the family circle: it was a three-sided receptacle for the body, and, had anybody thought of it, might have given rise to a saying complementary to 'an Englishman's house is his castle', so that we could have said, 'an Englishman's chair is his cabin'. You retired into your chair, and only extended into the outer world the stem of your long clay pipe and your legs from the knees downward. You retired to sit upright, for the chair-backs were straight although upholstered.

In the forty years between 1660 and 1700 the settle underwent a change. Its form remained, but its high back and arms were swaddled with upholstery, while the supporting framework of its long seat developed an ornamental character, the knees of the legs bent gently in scrolls, an anticipation of the true sweeping cabriole curve that was to come later. The stretchers that linked the legs in front, arched upwards to meet the underframe of the seat; and this combination of carved walnut and rich brocade or velvet became the high-backed settee, companion to the wing chair, another competent barrier to draughts. A compact and intimate invention was the love-seat; an appropriate product of Charles II's reign, though the term is modern. This was a small upholstered settee for two people sitting side by side.

There was also the day-bed, a long seat with an adjustable head that could be lowered so it became an extension of the seat. Both seat and head were usually of cane-work. The framework would have arched stretchers, extravagantly carved, and scroll legs, while the head would be framed with twisted or turned vertical uprights with carved cresting at the top.

Chair-makers were borrowing ideas from Spain and from Portugal. Cabinet-makers were borrowing ideas

FIG. 38. William and Mary walnut marquetry cabinet.
FIG. 39. Walnut chest on stand, c. 1690.
FIG. 40. Black lacquer cabinet on carved and gilded wood stand, c. 1675–80.
FIGS. 41, 42. Walnut marquetry long-case clock, and bed completely covered in fabric. Late XVIIth century.
FIG. 43. Walnut table, c. 1695. Gilt mirror, c. 1700.

63

from Holland and from China. Only in the country was there a true national expression of design, and various localities made characteristic types of furniture. To-day regional labels are too confidently applied to examples of Puritan design, such as chairs with turned legs and open backs with carved crescent-shaped cross rails linking the vertical members. (Pages 3 and 55, Fig. 20.) Another type, sometimes associated with Derbyshire and Lancashire, had instead of an open back a solid panel with a semicircle of carved cresting above. Sometimes that solid panel would be carved in low relief. (Fig. 19, page 55.)

The impress of the English craftsman's gift for making a comely statement of fitness was beginning to fade from town-made furniture. Mr. Pepys was noting examples of rich and unusual furnishing, and as early as 1660 (19th October) he records the brave setting he had ordered for his own dining-room furniture: 'This morning my dining-room was finished with greene serge hanging and gilt leather, which is very handsome'.

On 29th May 1694 he describes the house of Mr. Povey: 'And in a word, methinks, for his perspective in the little closet; his room floored above with woods of several colours, like but above the best cabinet-work I ever saw; his grotto and vault, with his bottles of wine, and a well therein to keep them cool; his furniture of all sorts; his bath at the top of the house, good pictures, and his manner of eating and drinking; do surpass all that ever I did see of one man in all my life'. Evelyn also refers to Mr. Povey's 'elegant house in Lincoln's-inn-fields' and was also impressed with 'the inlaying of his closet' (1st July 1664).

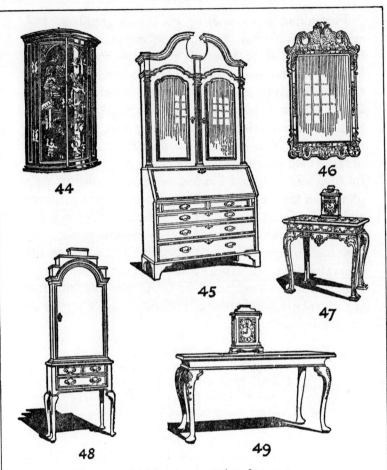

FIG. 44. Black lacquer hanging corner cupboard, c. 1720.
FIG. 45. Walnut bureau cabinet, c. 1710.
FIGS. 46, 47. Mirror with gilt gesso frame, bracket clock, and gilt gesso table, early XVIIIth century.
FIG. 48. Walnut cabinet with china display shelves, early XVIIIth century.
FIG. 49. Walnut table with marble top, c. 1720, and lacquer clock, c. 1735.

6

Furnishing was acquiring conscious grandeur, and again the craftsman and his native ideas were submerged. This time, however, patronage was educated. Fashion was not being flaunted and controlled by a new rich class, a mercantile aristocracy which could not appreciate good proportion. The outrages upon form that had characterised the previous Stuart period were not repeated. Now fashion was under the control of men of taste, men who had cultivated their regard for beautiful things in Italy and France, versatile gentlemen who gloried in their knowledge of architecture and painting and music, for in those days it was not considered a disadvantage to be a cultivated and intelligent person. No fool had invented the term 'highbrow' to excuse his own inferiority. Sometimes love of elegant surroundings went to a man's head, and Charles Cotton has some fun at the expense of this type of affliction in his *Epigram de Mons. Maynard*:

> Anthony feigns him Sick of late,
>     Only to shew how he at home,
> Lies in a Princely Bed of State,
>     And in a nobly furnish'd Room
> Adorned with pictures of Vandike's,
>     A pair of Chrystal Candlesticks,
> Rich Carpets, Quilts, the Devil, and all:
>     Then you, his careful Friends if ever
> You wish to cure him of his Fever,
>     Go lodge him in the Hospital.

But all these gentlemen and ladies who surrounded themselves with beautiful things had an eye for good design. Their furniture was ornate; but it was never stupidly ornate. Its decoration was never allowed to destroy its structural good sense. Chairs remained

66

chairs; they were not, as French craftsmen made them later, mere excuses for ornamentation, so that an article that was primarily a seat became a rococo extravaganza upon which it was almost impossible to sit. English furniture did not degenerate in this way, and florid though it might be, the furniture of the Carolean period had dignity and beauty. (See oyster-wood chest, Plate V, and walnut armchair, Plate XIII.)

There were great increases in convenience. Looking-glasses were no longer rare and exceptional articles; now their steel-coloured glass everywhere provided dark pools of reflection, usually set in wide walnut frames. Later in the seventeenth century mirrors were edged with bands of blue glass. Clocks were also becoming commoner. Little brass chamber clocks with bells, lantern, bedpost or bird-cage as they are now called, had come into general use during the seventeenth century. The early lantern clocks had domed bells with decorative finials surmounting their brass cases, and they hung or stood on a bracket on the wall, with their weights depending from chains or cords. Before the Restoration the pendulum was introduced, and these hanging clocks were provided with wooden cases and presently the pendulum was also enclosed in wood so that the whole interior mechanism was protected by a timber integument, and the long-case clock was in being.

Chests were now raised on legs and consisted of two, three or four sets of drawers, the drawer fronts being elaborately moulded, and the legs of the stand twisted. Decorative lacquer cabinets were imported from China and were provided with intricately carved stands which were gilded or silvered. The rudimentary cabriole form was employed for the legs of these stands; the inevitable amorini lurked in their leafy scrolls, and two totally dissimilar forms of decoration were often appropriately united by that all-saving sense of proportion which was the happy possession of Carolean designers. Many of these lacquer cabinets were imported, and from Holland the wooden carcases of chests, bureaux and tables were shipped to the East where they were lacquered and decorated by Chinese artists and returned to Europe. Attempts to imitate Chinese lacquer were made both on the Continent and in England, generally with unsatisfactory results, for a depressing muddiness frequently marred the colour, and the decoration itself was often ill-placed, and lacked the vigour and skill of Chinese decorators.

When the Stuart period ended in the revolution of 1688, Dutch taste became powerful once again, and with it came the extensive introduction of marquetry furniture. A good definition of marquetry is given in H. P. Shapland's *Practical Decoration of Furniture*:[1] 'Strictly speaking, inlaid work should be regarded as the technique which consists of forming slight sinkings of an eighth or quarter of an inch deep in the solid wood, and then filling the hollows so made with woods of a different colour, cut to fit them. Marqueterie is a later development and is closely bound up with veneering. In marqueterie the ornament is first cut into a thin sheet of wood or veneer and subsequently the veneer and ornament, as one sheet, are applied to the surface of the wood.' It was an entirely foreign importation. Veneered marquetry, as Mr. R. W. Symonds points out, 'had no period of evolution or transition in England; it was

[1] Vol. i, Section 2, p. 17.

a Dutch craft brought into this country in a fully developed state'.[1]

The William and Mary period was one of transition. The profusion of late Stuart decoration disappeared and was replaced by surface decoration that indicated a growing sense of texture. Such appreciation of texture had never before been apparent in English furniture-making. All the early inlaid work showed a disregard for richness and variety of surface. It was really only the crude insertion of different materials into a wooden base, and from Elizabethan times until the end of the Carolean period, ebony, ivory, mother-of-pearl, holly, sycamore and various other decorative materials were thrust into receptive hollows in the fronts of chests. It was only when the delicate and beautiful craft of veneering was practised in England that inlaid work acquired such refinements as oyster-wood decoration, which is found on Carolean and William and Mary table-tops, chests and cabinets.[2] Possibly the taste for Oriental things increased the appreciation for decorative surfaces.

All the furniture of the William and Mary period has a crisp, definite line, a sureness of touch in decoration, and is beginning to suggest the dignity of contemporary building. The large state beds that were designed with their posts concealed by curtains, and enormous testers with deep valances depending from a decorative cornice, were wholly architectural in form, reflecting, with appropriate consideration for the nature of the materials used, the bland, gentlemanly architecture that was taking shape in brick and stone all over England.[3]

[1] R. W. Symonds, *Old English Walnut and Lacquer Furniture*, chap. **v**, p. 87.

[2] See Plate **V**.          [3] See Fig. 42, p. 63.

The most spectacular piece of rebuilding that had been done in the last third of the seventeenth century was in London after the Great Fire; and because of that great architectural effort, we are sometimes liable to forget how much rebuilding of towns was going on throughout England, sometimes under the direction of great London architects, sometimes demonstrating the fertile talent of some local genius, like Henry Bell of Lynn, who largely rebuilt that little jewel of a town, then a great port on the Wash, and still lovely to-day despite the savage mutilations occasioned by local ignorance during the last half-century. Town houses and country houses were being rebuilt or pulled down and started again from new foundations. There was little tenderness for existing structures. We find Evelyn in 1671 (17th October) commenting on a Ducal Palace to which he paid a visit: 'It is an old wretched building, and that part of it newly built of brick is very ill-understood, so as I was of opinion it had been much better to have demolished all, and set it up in a better place, than to proceed farther'. The year before, he mentions Lord Alington's house (20th August 1670): 'We went to dine at Lord Alington's, he had newly built a house of great cost, I believe little less than £20,000. His architect was Mr. Pratt.'

By the end of the seventeenth century upholstered furniture was comparatively common. The easy-chair, the settee, cane-backed single and elbow chairs, and upholstered stools all afforded soft and yielding seats supported on turned legs which were linked by decorative underframing. Cabinets and chests on stands in walnut, in lacquer, in marquetry, had gradually raised the level of accommodation. There were more pieces of

Two examples of comb-back Windsor chairs with cabriole legs: mid-eighteenth and early nineteenth century.

Hoop-back Windsor chairs, with spur stretchers. Mid-eighteenth and early nineteenth century. Such chairs were manufactured extensively in the English North American colonies during the eighteenth century: the comb-back type was generally preferred, with regional variations of design. (See page 73.)

furniture that stood at or above the level of a man's head, while the long-case clock rose above it. Tables had increased in variety and mechanical efficiency. There were tables with drawers in them, single leaf and double leaf gate-leg tables, tables with draw-out tops and with all manner of decorative elaborations in the shape of veneered surfaces and marquetry and oyster-wood inlay.

Early eighteenth-century furniture showed that English makers had digested a fresh set of foreign ideas satisfactorily. In the period, somewhat loosely described as 'Queen Anne', the blending of Dutch influences upon form and decoration with the English craftsman's common-sense approach to problems of bearing weight or providing accommodation resulted in furniture of noble proportions. Not only in the most fashionable form of furniture, but in the simplest things made in the countryside, a new sensitivity to good proportion and a new understanding of structural possibilities became apparent. In the country, for example, a chair was invented that was perfectly adjusted to the needs of the human body, employing with gracious economy the minimum amount of material needed for securing the maximum of stability and comfort. It was produced in unconscious accordance with the functionalist doctrines of our own century; and was of stick construction. The seat was shaped from a clay mould that had accurately recorded a comfortable posture. The rake of the back was suited to an attitude of ease. The legs were sturdy and reliable. The name Windsor, now a generic name for these chairs, has been traced back as early as 1724. In 1728 it appears in a catalogue of the furniture of Thomas Coke, sold on 12th February in the Great

Piazza, Covent Garden. There are two basic types: the hoop-back and the comb-back.

The Windsor chair followed the English tradition of woodworking. When it was evolving, the chair-makers of London were obediently bending their knees in

*Left*: A form of Windsor chair known as a Smoker's Bow, first made during the second quarter of the nineteenth century. The name was probably derived from the bow-shaped back and the widespread use of the type in smoking-rooms and inn parlours.

*Right*: A variation of the Windsor type, known as a Mendlesham or Dan Day chair, said to have been originated in the early nineteenth century by Daniel Day of Mendlesham and Stoneham in Suffolk.

deference to a new fashion. The cabriole leg everywhere made courteous inclinations in English rooms. The swelling outward curve and the subtle concave inward bend below it, terminating in a shapely foot, became popular in England round about 1700 as a chair-leg and table-leg form. Although it was not invented in Holland it gained most of its refinements there. The scroll leg that was used on Carolean furniture was

73

a rather unwieldy forerunner of the cabriole, and in some of the elaborately carved stands for lacquer cabinets which were perhaps the most florid expressions of English baroque in the time of Charles II, there is again a hint of those counterbalancing curves, the heavy convex dominating above easing down into the slender concave curve below. There is in the Victoria and Albert Museum a lacquer chest on an exceptionally ornate stand. The four legs consist in the upper part of armless amorini gazing from the four corners of the stand with concentrated fatuity of expression. These little monsters have protuberant bellies and they are legless, becoming in the lower regions decorative mermen as it were, their gross bodies being supported upon an inward curving stem of writhing acanthus leaves. This sort of thing was made about 1680. In Germany, where grossness in decoration, and in everything else, has always won approval, such turgescent, ill-proportioned rubbish was produced even in the eighteenth century. In a way, those bloated little cupids, so aggressively mutilated, anticipated the cabriole-leg form. But the idea of the cabriole leg is older than the seventeenth century. It can be seen on the exquisite bronze furniture in the Naples Museum that has been removed from Pompeii. It is derived from a conventional representation of an animal's leg. In that Roman furniture of the first and second centuries A.D. may be found some of the familiar features of the Queen Anne and Early Georgian periods. The claw and hoof feet of tables are there rendered in metal or stone. The progress of the paw foot for chairs may be traced from ancient Egypt down to the French Empire furniture of Napoleon.

The cabriole leg appeared not only on chairs and

tables, but on stands, bureaux, stools and settees. It passed through a florid and uncertain transitional phase in the William and Mary period when the scroll form complicated its lines, and the free placing of chair feet was muddled by diagonal stretchers, or stretchers linking the front and back legs of a chair with another horizontal tie uniting them below the chair seat. It was not until the reign of Queen Anne that the cabriole leg in its pure form emerged and chair-makers dispensed with underframing and the stretcher disappeared, leaving a graceful piece of furniture, bold and flowing in its lines, simple and strong in its construction, and endowed with an air of civilised graciousness that reflected improved manners.[1] Instead of the rather tortuous collection of framed cane-work, upright members, twisted bars and heavily carved cresting, that appeared in the backs of the late Stuart chairs, the simple types of the early eighteenth century had a broad, shapely central splat, linking the seat with the top rail, and two gently curving outer vertical members. (Plate XIII.)

Elaborate forms of furniture such as the bureau and bureau-bookcase and the knee-hole writing-desk were now made. They suggested the growing power architectural forms had over the work of cabinet-makers. The bureau-bookcase would rise to the ceiling like some miniature building. Its upper part would be flanked with fluted pilasters surmounted by a cornice with a pediment above. There was real kinship between these great pieces of furniture and the buildings that Wren and Gibbs and Hawksmoor and Vanbrugh were design-

[1] There is a theory that stretchers were retained on chairs to enable people to keep their shoes from contact with the unsavoury rush-strewn floor. Floors, if the frankness of Mr. Pepys means anything, could not have been very pleasant, whether rushes were used or not, in the seventeenth century.

ing. Men who had executed interior woodwork for the great architects of the time would be well drilled in proportion, and they would apply their knowledge when they returned to cabinet-making. Some of the long-case clocks recall by their proportion and their easy ascending lines the steeples of Wren's churches.[1] The affinity between architectural forms and furniture design everywhere became clearer as the eighteenth century advanced. Even on mirror frames the disposition of ornament and the proportions suggested architectural features. The architect designed the background for furniture, and inevitably furniture-makers were employed to produce things that harmonised with the panelling, the chimney-pieces, the enriched cornices and door and window architraves.

In Charles II's reign Mr. Evelyn had discovered and Sir Christopher Wren had employed Grinling Gibbons, a carver with a great capacity for creating florid and beautifully fluent decoration. He embellished furniture and mirror frames and architectural woodwork in churches, private houses and public buildings. Some of this carved decoration was beautiful, and when architects of the calibre of Sir Christopher Wren were in control of its placing it was wonderfully effective. But it was inclined to overpower furniture. Grinling Gibbons and the carvers who were inspired by his work did not reduce the scale of their ornament sufficiently. They were called upon to decorate furniture. In the process they hatched a hideous brood of adipose cupids.

Early in the eighteenth century a material called gesso was employed. It was a composition used as a coating on the woodwork of tables, mirror frames, chairs

[1] See Plate XVI.

76

and cabinets. It consisted of whitening and size, and successive layers of it built up on a wood ground could be carved into the most soft and flowing lines. The bulgings and thrustings of the Grinling Gibbons school were replaced by softer and more subtle ornament, and this delicate work was usually gilded. Although gesso was not used extensively until the reign of Queen Anne, it was actually introduced from Italy late in the seventeenth century.

For nearly two decades, after 1700, English furniture again achieved rich and satisfying harmonies of form. All the foreign influences of the late Stuart and William and Mary periods had been assimilated; once again English furniture was national, and therefore simple. It was dignified too, in a new and gracious way. But not for long did it keep its purity of form, its freedom from ornamental complexities. The early Georgian period began badly. Court taste drew its ideas from Germanic sources and the results were unfortunate: the influence of a royal mistress was painfully apparent. The Duchess of Kendal, who was honoured by the warm friendship of George I, distinguished herself by arranging for the dismissal of Sir Christopher Wren from the office of surveyor-general, possibly because he did not see eye to eye with her about her schemes for the alteration of Hampton Court. George I dismissed Wren and conferred his office upon a brainless nonentity called Benson. This is an interesting example of the treatment almost invariably accorded to the great designers England produces; but bad Court taste and the whims of harlots could not destroy the influence of England's great architects nor debilitate the educated taste of the nobility and gentry. The influence of the

Court was not deeply marked, and although Germanic ideas affected the embellishment of furniture between 1715 and 1730—which could be described as the early Georgian period—the researches and travels of such noblemen as the Earl of Burlington and his capacity for enlightened patronage were far more potent factors in the moulding of contemporary taste.

The Earl of Burlington published the designs of Inigo Jones and Palladio's drawings of the 'Antiquities of Rome'. He was the discoverer and patron of William Kent, the decorator-architect who was one of the few people capable of designing extremely florid decoration that was well proportioned. (See Plates XIV and XV.)

Respect for common sense is deeply ingrained in the English character. It has in due time conquered every fashion, and after the beginning of the eighteenth century its power remained unbroken for one hundred and thirty years. Foreign influence, introduced once again by George I, had lost its power of completely upsetting English design and retarding its development. Everywhere at this time common sense was triumphant in the shaping of furniture. Everywhere cabinet-makers and chair-makers were studying architectural forms. Mahogany, a new and beautiful material, had been introduced, and it replaced walnut as walnut had replaced oak, except in the countryside, where ash, beech, oak, yew, elm, cherry and apple wood were used for simplified versions of town-made things.

The new curvilinear conception of chair design which came in with the eighteenth century destroyed the rigid dignity of chairs. Comfort was on the way: chairs were no longer frames for the formal stiffness of posture that distinguished ladies and gentlemen of the sixteenth and seventeenth centuries. The upright lines of the Puritan and Carolean chairs still had obvious affinities with the box-like chairs of an earlier age (see Plates XII and XIII), and were indeed more closely related to them than to the gracious early Georgian types on this page. *Above, left*: An elbow chair, with a 'bended-back', scroll-over arms, cabriole legs and claw-and-ball feet. *Above, right*: Elbow chair of the same period, with stuffed seat and back. *Below, left*: Side view of the curves in a scroll-over arm. *Drawn by Marcelle Barton.*

*Above*: A serpentine-fronted chest with straight wings and bracket feet.
*Below, left*: A sheveret, also described as a lady's cabinet. *Right*: A lady's
work-table, which was a miniature form of sheveret. Reproduced from
*The Prices of Cabinet Work*, 1797 edition.

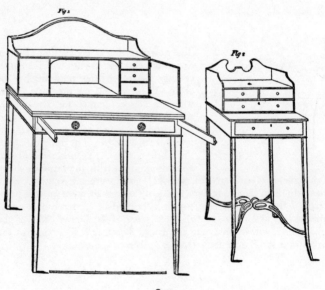

CHAPTER V

# FURNITURE DESIGN UNDER THE
## ARCHITECTS, 1730–1830

CLIVE BELL, in his essay, *Civilisation*, observes
that: 'The eighteenth century understood the importance of art; and its taste, though limited, was pure
enough. In the minor and domestic arts it could dis-
criminate finely; and the rich were willing to pay for
beauty not in cash only but in time and trouble. The
rich men and women of the eighteenth century cultivated their taste.' These sentences refer more specifically
to French society of that period, but they are applicable
also to England, where patronage had attained levels
of education and intelligence that made it possible for
the design of everything to be subjected to a critical
scrutiny that was based upon a genuine perception of
excellence in proportion and appropriateness in ornamentation. No architect was perplexed by the ignorant
repetition of that Philistine phrase: 'I know what I like!'
A gentleman knew when anything was well or ill proportioned; he understood that great system of horizontal and vertical rhythms and of surface variation and
relief and adornment which the talented architects of
the time had erected upon a sound Vitruvian foundation.
He could discuss design with designers as a technical
equal. And for the stimulation of his taste and for the
better information of the humbler people who ministered
to it, architects, and presently furniture-makers, began
to write books on design.

81                                                    7

In 1739 William Jones, architect, published and sold at his house ('near the Chapple in King Street, Golden Square') a bound collection of copper-plate engravings entitled: *The Gentlemens or Builders Companion, Containing Variety of usefull Designs for Doors, Gateways, Peers, Pavilions, Temples, Chimney-pieces, Slab Tables, Pier Glasses, or Tabernacle Frames, Ceiling Pieces, &c.* It was a slim book in which no type was used; even the title-page and contents-table were engraved on copper plates; and the designs on those plates suggest that they were an architect's rough notes for the guidance of his own drawing-office rather than models for public consumption. There are a few undistinguished chimney-pieces, several mirror frames of good proportion, mostly with triangular pediments above friezes embellished with masks and swags. Six plates are given to marble-topped tables with legs and frames that are shaggy with carving, although the ornament is well placed. There is one grotesque table with the legs ending in hoof feet, with sad-looking, heavily whiskered masks just above them, whose beards stray down over the hooves. The various architectural details are in what Wren would have called 'a good Roman manner'; but the designs in this handbook on ornament and furniture that was published in the eighteenth century are blameless rather than inspiring. Batty Langley, who was a writing as well as a practising architect, published *The Builder's and Workman's Treasury of Designs: or the Art of Drawing and Working The Ornamental Parts of Architecture.* 400 'grand designs' on 186 copper-plates.[1]

---

[1] The publication date of the copy in the Library of the Royal Institute of British Architects is 1750, but many of the plates in it had an earlier distribution, and are dated 1739.

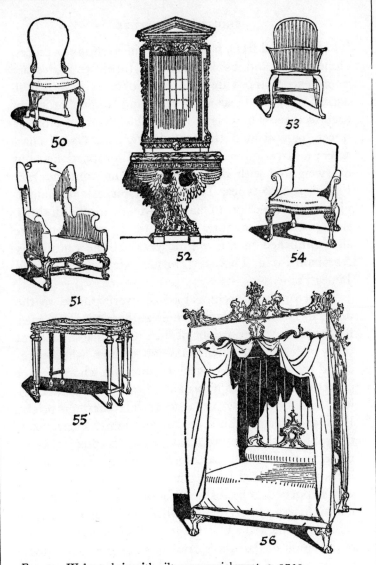

FIG. 50. Walnut chair with gilt gesso enrichment, c. 1730.
FIG. 51. Gilt gesso easy-chair covered in velvet, c. 1740.
FIG. 52. Gilt mirror, c. 1740. Gilt console table, c. 1735.
FIG. 53. Early XVIIIth-century Windsor armchair.
FIG. 54. Armchair in mahogany with gilt enrichment, c. 1725.
FIGS. 55, 56. Mahogany centre table with fretted gallery, and Chippendale mahogany bed, c. 1745–60.

They included frets, tabernacle frames, chimney-pieces, stone tables and bookcases. The furniture plates are poor, except those devoted to bookcases designed to accord with the Tuscan, 'Dorick' and 'Ionick' orders of architecture. There is a regrettable dressing-table; a queer, complicated chest of drawers, of Dutch character; and various table frames, well-proportioned but overweighted with ornament and aping contemporary French rococo types. The chimney-pieces and mantel-pieces are superior to any of the furniture designs. Books on architectural design and ornament were also published in the middle years of the century by Abraham Swan, Thomas Johnson, Matthias Lock and James Paine.

Most of these technical books were guides to the detail of classic ornament; their authors set forth rules for the correct proportions of the orders of architecture; their plates imparted information to men who appreciated the orderliness of architecture and who were not content merely to copy ornament out of a book. England had become sensitive to architectural propriety. Even the village cabinet-maker and joiner knew something about the five orders; and they wanted to know more, for patrons were more exacting. The squire's ideas were affected by the taste of the great nobleman who happened to be his neighbour and whose ancestral mansion was either being pulled down or extensively rebuilt in the Palladian manner. Pope's apprehension of the result of Palladio's drawings being published was partly justified. But those 'noble rules' Burlington revealed to England, while impelling a few 'imitating fools' to rush to their aesthetic doom, did strengthen the desire to comprehend the spirit of architectural design and to master its principles and then to achieve good proportion in all things, not only among architects, but among country builders and wood-workers, masons, joiners, smiths and cabinet-makers.

There was a willingness to accept architectural dictatorship in design; very different from the surly submission of resentful Tudor craftsmen to foreign ideas. Architects, like Isaac Ware, who published a book called *The Complete Body of Architecture*, extended that exacting control over the interior of the houses they designed that was to culminate in the work of the brothers Adam, and which survived in the early nineteenth century in the work of Thomas Hope. Isaac Ware's book was 'adorned with Plans and Elevations from Original Designs' and included 'some designs by Inigo Jones never before published'. The whole seemly background of contemporary life as the architect would have it was revealed in measured detail in 122 plates and 10 books. It well deserved the word 'complete', this rich amplification of Vitruvius, for it was a fool-proof guide for everyone who worked in stone or brick or wood, and it dealt intimately with materials. There were chapters on timber, on oak and fir, when it should be felled, how it should be used, and a table of useful timber trees.[1] In the preface Ware shows that architects were accepting their wide responsibility for design, and incidentally condenses the English point of view about architecture into this sentence: 'Architecture has been celebrated as a noble science by many who have never regarded its benefits in common life: we have endeavoured to join these several parts of the subject, nor shall we fear to say that the art of building cannot be

[1] Book I, chaps. xvi to xxi.

85

more grand than it is useful; nor its dignity a greater praise than its convenience'. Ware built Chesterfield House for Philip Earl of Chesterfield.

William Kent, under the patronage of the Earl of Burlington, not only designed buildings and interior decoration, but designed furniture of an ornate kind. It was an age of generous and emphatic but never inappropriate ornament. The cabriole legs of chairs and tables were lavishly adorned with gilded carving. Mouldings were enriched and gilded on the cornices and pediments of bureaux and cabinets. The edges of tables and desks were scalloped with nulling, heavily gilded. Fluting was gilded. The carved knees of chairs were gilded. Claw-and-ball and hoof feet were gilded. Rooms were warm with aureate high-lights. Orderly extravagance reigned: masks, shells, scroll-work, swags of fruit and flowers, trophies and cornucopia, festoons and ribbons and miles of egg-and-dart enrichment deployed in disciplined formations across every surface. The massing of ornament, its disposition and grouping were decided with a sureness of touch and a sureness of taste that had never before enlivened any phase of elaboration in English furnishing or interior decoration. Compare with this surety of judgement the decorative chaos of the Edwardian period. Mr. Roger Fry in *Vision and Design* describes in detail a room that was quite as elaborate as any room in a wealthy gentleman's house in the second, third or fourth decade of the eighteenth century; it was a railway refreshment-room, and its decoration and furnishing had commanded materials and mechanical processes unknown in the early Georgian period, and all those materials and processes were misused with vapid brutality to create an

57        58        59

60        61        62

63        64        65

FIGS. 57, 58, 59. Ladderback chair, Chinese Chippendale settee and Chippendale type chair, c. 1740–60.

FIGS. 60, 61, 62. Adam furniture: inlaid mahogany chair, silk-covered painted settee, and carved mahogany chair, c. 1760–90.

FIGS. 63, 64, 65. Hepplewhite furniture: armchair with Prince of Wales feathers in back, settee in mahogany with four conjoined shield-shaped chair backs, and chair with heart-shaped back. (See also page 111.)

effect of richness. Mr. Fry's patient inventory of the ornamentation and contents of that room makes us recall many similar exhibitions of ungoverned profusion. To quote only three sentences from his essay is enough to give a cutting edge to a comparison of the period 1900–1914 with the seventeen-twenties and -thirties. 'On the walls, up to a height of four feet, is a covering of lincrusta walton stamped with a complicated pattern in two colours, with sham silver medallions. Above that a moulding but an inch wide, and yet creeping throughout its whole with a degenerate descendant of a Graeco-Roman carved guilloche pattern; this has evidently been cut out of the wood by machine or stamped out of some composition—its nature is so perfectly concealed that it is hard to say which. Above this is a wall-paper in which an effect of eighteenth-century satin brocade is imitated by shaded staining of the paper.'[1] Mr. Fry attributes 'this eczematous eruption of pattern on the surface of modern manufactures' to the fact that the business of the hack draughtsmen employed by manufacturers 'is to produce, not expressive design, but dead patterns'. 'Dead patterns' were produced in the early seventeenth century, before patronage was educated in design or executant craftsmen understood the principles of architectural composition: 'dead patterns' appeared in the nineteenth century and lived on into the twentieth because patronage was ignorant and even architects had forgotten—and had, indeed, been urged to forget by John Ruskin—the principles of architectural composition.[2]

[1] From the essay on *Art and Socialism*, originally written in 1912.

[2] '. . . whatever betrays the smallest respect for Vitruvian laws or conformity with Palladian work—that we are to endure no more' (*The Stones of Venice*, vol. iii, chap. 4).

Throughout the eighteenth century, with architects as directors of taste and design working for educated patrons, no experiment in profusion, no gay rococo antics, resulted in vulgarity or 'dead patterns'. No matter what particular foible of fashion was being accommodated by furniture-makers, good sturdy common sense never allowed the structural bones of furniture to be malformed. Architectural knowledge shaped everything that went into the house of the eightenth-ceentury gentleman. His candlesticks, his door-knocker, his fireplace furniture and the legs of his easy-chair exactly accorded with the character of the panelling on his walls and the design of his chimney-piece. When he sat in his study or library, wherever his eye fell, he could be certain of seeing comely and gracious things. Nothing jarred upon him. Every article was adjusted to suit his habits, his convenience, his manners and his clothes. For example, the arms of chairs were set back a little from the front of the seat in consideration of the broad skirted coats worn by gentlemen and the spreading pannier skirts of the ladies. Tables of every description were made, tables that were mere ornamental side-pieces, card-tables, occasional-tables, tripod-tables and the most ample and elegant dining-tables.

By the middle of the eighteenth century nearly every article of furniture was made in mahogany. Walnut survivals are found sometimes as late as 1730–40, but English walnut was not used extensively after about 1725. Virginia walnut was sometimes imported from America, and this dark wood which takes on a reddish hue in time, is often mistaken for mahogany. (Mr. R. W. Symonds in his book *English Furniture from*

*Charles II to George II* illustrates a chest with drawers with a folding top, made in solid Virginia walnut about 1720, on page 123.) Plate XVI shows a small table of Queen Anne type in Virginia walnut. Mahogany gave the English furniture-maker a lovely material; he appreciated its beauties and seldom concealed the glowing wood with painting or gilding in the manner of Continental makers. The character of wood as a material has always appealed to the English craftsman, and although he has used gilding and inlay he has never allowed embellishment to compete with the colour and texture of his basic material. The direction of furniture design by architects never deranged the craftsman's ability to use to the utmost decorative advantage the natural beauty of wood.

On Plate XVI a long case clock in figured walnut is shown, which derives much of its decorative character from the skilful choosing of veneers for the base and for the door of the case. The mouldings on the base and those used at the junction of the case and the head gain a subtle emphasis by reason of thoughtfully picked walnut for their surfaces. The whole of this design exemplifies a studied selection of materials to accord with proportions. In the period in which this clock was produced, it was the fashion to depend largely upon the character of wood for decoration. It was an age of great accomplishment in veneering, in the choosing and matching of colour and figure, in the contrivance of agreeable contrasts in the markings of walnut, and the attainment of delicate accentuations for structural lines.

The English makers' regard for the nature of wood survives every alteration of mode. Consider the Georgian

Fig. 66. (right) A painted pier table and glass with gilt frame, c. 1785. Although there is an abundance of delicate ornamentation on both table and frame, severity of line is preserved which is typical of the work of Robert Adam.

Fig. 67. (below) An Adam sideboard with pedestals, painted and gilded. See also bed and sideboard on Plate XXIII.

91

chest shown in Plate XVIII. Observe the disposition of the ornament, used only on those parts that offer the minimum amount of surface for the display of the colour and marking of the mahogany from which the chest is constructed. The drawer front is broken only by three functional features—the two drawer-handles and the lock-plate. Above the drawer is a plain expanse of smokily figured mahogany with one bright functional feature in the upper part, namely the lock-plate. The front of the stand has only one piece of carving, the inverted shell, and the legs with their lightly carved acanthus scrolls springing from rosettes and branching out over the knees ascend into the plain stand framework, and the contrast with a stretch of unadorned surface stresses their fluent lines.

Plate XXI again attests the English maker's sense of touch with wood. The mahogany press there illustrated is essentially an architectural piece. Every line certifies the lessons that had been learnt throughout all England from the proportions of classic architecture. Such furniture by its character suggests a common understanding of the fact that 'Rome was glorious, not profuse. . . .' Reticence in the treatment of any design could hardly be better demonstrated than in the shape and embellishment of this press. The figured mahogany contributes its colour and marking, unspoiled by the intrusive rivalry of extraneous carving or the application of any feature that could detract from the natural amplitude of its beauty. The carved mask is a focal point, terminating the vertical line that divides the cupboard doors, completing the unifying effect already begun by the unbroken horizontal lines of the two bottom drawers of the base, preventing any suggestion of 'an unresolved duality'.[1] The only other carving is upon the four claw-footed legs.

On Plate XVII another mahogany press shows an even stronger imprint of architectural taste. This piece is influenced by the work of Batty Langley. Books and plates like those published by Batty Langley and his brother Thomas, dealing with architectural design, were part of the equipment of the cabinet-maker's workshop and drawing-office when this press was made. But no amount of guidance and authoritative influence regarding the relative proportions of plinth, column and entablature with its architrave, frieze and cornice, could deflect the English cabinet-maker's interest from displaying the material he was using, and from producing something that was fit for its purpose.

Long before Horace Walpole extended the fashion for the Gothic taste, Batty Langley had published his *Gothic Architecture, Improved by Rules and Proportions, In many Grand Designs of Columns, Doors, Windows, Chimney-pieces, Arcades, Colonades, Porticos, Umbrellos, Temples and Pavillions, etc. with Plans, Elevations and Profiles, Geometrically Expressed.*[2] These solemn creations might have done infinite harm in any age less certain of and happy in its taste. Horace Walpole condemned Batty Langley's 'services' to Gothic architecture, observing that his books had only taught 'carpenters to massacre that venerable species. . . .' But in the middle years of the eighteenth century, it was diffi-

---

[1] The classification of certain architectural forms as 'unresolved dualities' has been made by Mr. A. Trystan Edwards in his book *The Things Which are Seen.* The west front of Cologne Cathedral is an unresolved duality; so is the Cathedral at Lucerne; so is a double-domed bureau bookcase; all have dominating twin vertical units, as subconsciously irritating to the eye as clashing colours.　　　　　　　[2] Published at 15s. in 1747.

cult for carpenters, cabinet-makers and chair-makers to be corrupted by any fashionable freak; it was unusual, too, for an architect to design anything clumsy or ungracious however queer or eccentric might be the dictatorship of a transitory mode. The sensitiveness of every architect, craftsman and patron to good proportion was too highly developed for ugliness to be imposed by any unusual experiment in mere novelty.

Mr. R. W. Symonds in that detailed account of the design, material and quality of workmanship in English walnut and mahogany furniture, already mentioned, *English Furniture from Charles II to George II*, writes: 'Not only did the old designers base the proportion of their pieces upon the classical orders, but they copied the sections of mouldings, and in many cases derived their ornament from classical examples. This close adherence in furniture design to architectural principles was specially prevalent in the first three quarters of the eighteenth century and particularly noticeable in such pieces as bookcases and cabinets. Designers in this period sometimes carried the adoption of architectural treatment to the absurd length of combining a bookcase with a structure of classical proportions with Chinese and Gothic *motifs*.'[1] Even when incongruous examples of architectural detail were incorporated, the cabinet-maker's sense of proportion restrained him from perpetrating the clumsy hybrid monsters that appeared in Victorian times, and although to the purist the spectacle of Gothic glazing bars in doors of a bookcase of classical proportions might be disturbing, it was an offence against academic scholarship, not against good proportion.

[1] Chap. i, p. 10.

Thomas Chippendale, in the concluding paragraph of the preface to his book *The Gentleman and Cabinet Maker's Director*, first published in 1754, said: 'Upon the whole I have given no design but what may be executed with advantage by the hands of a skilled workman, tho' some of the profession have been diligent enough to represent them (especially those after the Gothic and Chinese manner) as so many specious drawings impossible to be worked off by any mechanic whatsoever. I will not scruple to attribute this to malice, ignorance and inability: And I am confident I can convince all Noblemen, Gentlemen, or others, who will honour me with their commands, that every design in the book can be improved, both as to beauty and enrichment in the execution of it, by their most obedient servant, Thomas Chippendale.' Only on rare occasions was Thomas Chippendale able to convince 'Noblemen, Gentlemen, or others' (architects are presumably included among 'others') that his Chinese and Gothic creations were not 'specious drawings'. Chippendale with a sheet of paper in front of him became repellently inventive; as ornate and disagreeably profuse as any French fashion-mongering cabinet-maker. It was seldom indeed that he was allowed to make in all their wild extravagance the abominable complexities that he illustrated in his book. But when he and his contemporaries were extravagant in the use of ornament, they never permitted such indulgence to weaken the structural integrity or debase the harmonious form of their furniture. An example of a richly ornamented chair of Chippendale type is shown on Plate XX. The legs, the back frame and the pierced back splat are all exquisitely carved in low relief. The stretchers in the underframing are pierced to correspond with the placing of the ornament on the seat frame and the legs. Here richness is gained without sacrifice of comfort or stability, without any touch of vulgarity, without gaudiness, without confusion.

By the time Chippendale was writing his book and taking orders from fashionable clients in his London shop in St. Martin's Lane, furniture had gained many new refinements of shape. The ponderousness of the early Georgian period had passed. The cabriole leg was still used, but with less frequency, and the straight leg or the tapering leg for chairs was commoner. The splats of chair-backs were pierced. The ladder-back chair was invented. Endless variations of treatment were created for the filling of chair-backs: sometimes they would accommodate Chinese frets, sometimes interlacing ribbons terminated in leafy scrolls of acanthus, as in the chair on Plate XX. The transition from the early Georgian chair to the more slender Chippendale type is shown on Plate XXII. The cabriole leg and the claw and ball foot are still retained; but a forecast of a later form is given by the back. (See also page 107.)

Four-post beds with light columns supporting delicate testers of fabric with gathered valances, replaced the massive state beds of the early eighteenth century. Plate XXIII indicates how much had been learned about shapeliness in bed design by the middle of the century. This plate shows a bed of Adam type in kingwood. The delicate twist of the posts is based on a classical model; the frieze with the Greek key pattern is already foreshadowing the development of painted furniture which was to be encouraged by the brothers Adam. It exhibits a new partnership between decorative

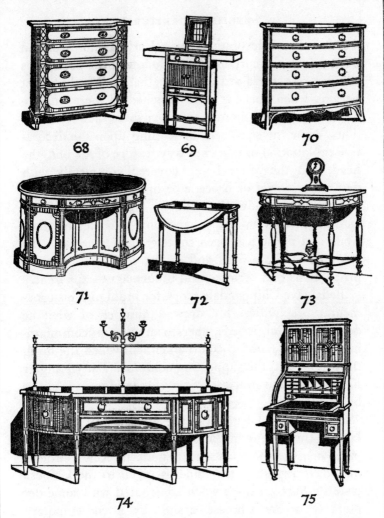

68     69     70

71     72     73

74     75

FIGS. 68, 69, 70. Mahogany inlaid chest of drawers, Shearer dressing chest with tambour front, and mahogany bow-fronted chest. Late XVIIIth century.

FIG. 71. Mahogany inlaid writing table.

FIG. 72. Hepplewhite mahogany inlaid Pembroke table.

FIG. 73. Balloon clock in mahogany, and satinwood side table. Early XIXth century.

FIG. 74. Shearer type of sideboard in mahogany and satinwood.

FIG. 75. Sheraton type satinwood bureau.

woodwork and decorative fabric. Early Tudor beds had
been frames for curtains. Then followed the ponderous
wooden structures of the Elizabethan and early Stuart
periods when curtains were attached as mere humble
fluttering rags to monumental expanses of woodwork.
Then came the state bed, depending upon the decorative exploitation of fabrics; every feature of the bed, the
head, and the tester being covered completely with
damask or velvet or brocade or brocatelle, without exposing any woodwork.[1] But by the middle of the
eighteenth century many handsome alliances between
wood and fabric had been contrived, and it was in the
columns of those beds and in the regulation of their
proportions that architectural influence was apparent.

Beds gave Chippendale scope for indulging his ornamental proclivities. He drew a number of what he
described as Gothic beds, wherein an unhappy commingl-
ing of Gothic and rococo ornament enlivened the head,
the canopy and the supporting columns. (Batty Langley
may have had as much to answer for as Horace Walpole
believed.)

Sir William Chambers, the architect of Somerset
House, the Albany in Piccadilly, and the little gem-like
pavilions, the orangery and pagoda in Kew Gardens,
may have regretted the impetus given to the Chinese
taste by his own work when confronted with some de-
plorably ornate Chinese design by a contemporary
cabinet-maker, for he had published in 1757 a treatise
on *Designs of Chinese Buildings, Furniture, Dresses,
Machines and Utensils*. This book revealed how his
imagination had been impressed by his travels in the
East; but when he experimented in some modified

---

[1] See Fig. 42 on p. 65.

form of Chinese design, as in the pagoda at Kew Gardens, he demonstrated how perfectly under the control of sound classical taste were these Oriental fancies, how gentlemanly, how correct they became when taught their manners and put through their paces by an accomplished architect. Even Mr. Chippendale, excellent and fashionable cabinet-maker though he was, found strong draughts of Oriental inspiration too much for his sense of proportion, which dissolved together with his sense of ornamental propriety whenever he was stimulated to design, on paper, something in the Chinese taste. He suggested not only Chinese beds, but Chinese sofas, most unhandy pieces of furniture, cumbered with canopies and overwhelmed with ornament. Unless Chippendale had come periodically under the discipline of architectural taste he might have injured his business by thrusting at his clients these complicated Chinese and Gothic experiments. He was employed by the brothers Adam to make furniture to their design. Few architects, and indeed few English ladies and gentlemen of that time, would have commissioned him to execute the wildest of the extravagances that appeared in the plates of *The Director*. The Gothic taste had to wait to be made fashionable by Horace Walpole; had to be chatted about by people who wanted to be in the mode, before it could grow and achieve such fantastic extravagance as William Beckford's Fonthill Abbey. It never seriously influenced the form of furniture in the eighteenth century, but, like the Chinese taste, inspired a few ornamental details, frets and so forth, some of which were agreeable enough. Whenever Chippendale attempted to make the queer things that he drew in *The Director*, his ability as a craftsman, his abundance of good English sense about

99

structure and form, saved him from producing what appears on paper to be meretricious and 'specious'.

Chippendale had opportunities for making elaborate decorative things, and his brackets, chimney-pieces, mirrors, picture frames, girandoles, fire-screens, pier glasses, torcheres, hanging book-shelves, stands for vases and so forth, displayed in many drawing-rooms, salons and boudoirs the effervescent gaiety of light, gilded carving. Chinese *motifs* supplied the theme for many of these fragile extravagances; but occasionally the design of a girandole was clearly taken from one of Piranesi's delineations of Roman ruins. A couple of solitary columns supporting a fragment of entablature would be counterbalanced by the remains of an arcade; a Chinese tree would grow through the ruins; perhaps an urn would mourn upon a pedestal; and, flowing in and out of the base of the design, the plastic coils of acanthus leaves would convey all the fluid extremes of rococo taste.

Contemporary with Chippendale were William Ince, Thomas Mayhew and Robert Manwaring. Ince and Mayhew had published *The Universal System of Household Furniture* whose plates included 300 designs of articles as varied as 'hall chairs, lanthorns, staircase lights, sideboards, claw tables, tea-kettle stands, book-cases, secretaires, library steps, writing-tables, music desks, canopy beds, French bed-chairs, dressing-tables, book and china shelves', etc. The book is undated but it was probably issued about 1762. In 1760 another volume on this subject appeared under the title of *Genteel Household Furniture in the Present Taste*, by the Society of Upholsterers. A second edition was called for, and in this chair designs by several makers appeared, among them work by Robert Manwaring, who republished twenty-eight of these designs in 1766, with forty-seven others, under the title of *The Chair Maker's Guide*. The additional plates were, almost all, ill drawn and poor in design. Manwaring had published a book of his own in 1765 called *The Cabinet and Chair Maker's Real Friend and Companion, or the whole system of chair-making made plain and easy*, in which chairs closely resembling those designed by Chippendale appeared in several of the plates.

Ince, Mayhew and Manwaring all made furniture of similar character to that designed by Chippendale; and Chippendale was not a great and solitary originator of an entirely fresh style; he was one of many successful tradesmen, skilfully supplying the needs of contemporary fashion in furniture design and making furniture of excellent quality. He died in 1779, and the type of furniture which he and his contemporaries made was replaced by another school of design, represented by the work of Richard Gillow, George Hepplewhite and Thomas Shearer. Chippendale had retained a certain squareness in the form of chairs, save in those types deliberately adapted from French models and labelled as such in the *Director*, and despite his ornamental outbreaks he preserved an affection for solidity and visible strength. Hepplewhite refined the form of furniture almost to the point of flimsiness. He is usually credited with the invention of the shield-back chair; but an inspection of the records of the firm of Gillow—which are preserved at the Lancaster branch of Waring and Gillow Ltd.—suggests that the originator of the design was Richard Gillow, to whom Hepplewhite had been apprenticed before he came to London.

This shield-shaped chair back was varied in form, sometimes being filled with splats, or with a vase motif in the centre (see page 111), or festoons, and occasionally the fluffy plumes of the Prince of Wales' feathers would be unfurled, or it was webbed with canework. Settees were formed by three or four conjoined shield-backs. Hepplewhite used the square-sectioned tapered, or Marlboro' leg, as it was called in the trade at that time. Legs were often turned, and were fluted or channelled and occasionally decorated with carved ornament in light relief. Hepplewhite also made elaborately fitted sideboards, though Shearer probably invented the sideboard in its form of a side table fitted with drawers and cupboards.

The brothers Adam designed painted furniture, chairs with small decorative plaques in the centre of the back, commodes in satinwood with panels painted thereon. They designed houses complete in every detail and they were meticulously correct in the ornament which they employed. Their work strongly influenced contemporary taste in furniture, and their designs caused cabinet-makers and chair-makers to explore many new ways of obtaining slender and delicate shapes. Robert Adam was the designer in this famous partnership. 'He reduced the refinement of architectural forms to a condition of frigid delicacy. Severe in outline, and painstakingly correct in every classical detail of their abundant and beautiful ornamentation, Adam's schemes were somewhat dehumanised. He designed houses complete with their contents, ordaining for ceilings and carpets, curtains, chair coverings and furniture the coldly elegant decoration that he pieced together from his profound knowledge of Greek and Roman ornament.

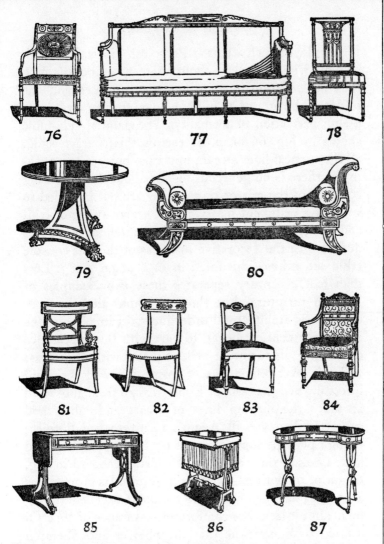

FIGS. 76, 77, 78. Satinwood chair with oval cane panel in back, settee and painted chair. Sheraton types, late XVIIIth century.

FIGS. 79, 80. Regency furniture: mahogany tripod table with brass mounts, and rosewood sofa with brass mounts.

FIGS. 81, 82. Rosewood chairs with inlaid brass lines.

FIGS. 83, 84. Rosewood chair with horsehair seat and carved chair with silk upholstery.

FIG. 85. Carved mahogany sofa table.   FIG. 86. Rosewood work table.

FIG. 87. Kidney-shaped writing table in satinwood.

He employed such artists as Pergolesi, Cipriani, Zucchi, and his wife, Angelica Kauffmann, to embellish with their little exquisite paintings the furniture and the rooms of the houses he built.'[1] Adam furniture achieves a slim perfection of formality. The painted side-table shown in Fig. 66 on p. 91 reveals this characteristic: all the vertical lines stream upwards, but not too gushingly; there is no generous vigour about the ascending columns of the mirror frame; they are not intended to support a pediment massive with hearty swags of fruit and flowers. Compare the exquisite attenuation of this design with the decorative lustiness of the gilt console table and mirror illustrated in Fig. 52 on p. 83. Less than half a century separates these two examples of English furniture, but the only thing they have in common is architectural orderliness. In its old age the eighteenth century began to part with the appearance of stability; its furniture-makers flirted with flimsiness; and this over-refinement of forms followed the staid interval when the taste of Robert Adam froze into rigid attitudes the flowing lines of chairs and tables and cabinets. And yet all Adam's furniture had dignity; though perhaps some of it was over-dignified, lean and stiff. Look at the painted and gilded sideboard in Fig. 67 on p. 91 with its guardian pedestals. Its proportions are noble; its ornamentation a tribute to excellent judgement; but it lacks the comfortable assurance of cheerful service at dinner-time that the Shearer and Sheraton types of sideboard (see Fig. 74, page 97, and example on page 113); the Adam sideboard suggests state occasions; the others suggest intimate and witty dinner parties.

[1] *Men and Buildings*, by John Gloag, chap. vii, p. 117 (1931 edition).

Although one of the effects of Robert Adam's taste was to increase the use of painted furniture, and although satinwood occasionally flashed its bright yellow surfaces in bedrooms and drawing-rooms and boudoirs, mahogany was still the principal furniture wood. The sort of mahogany used in the eighteenth century is now unobtainable, for it was cut near the coast in the West Indies, coming generally from San Domingo and the Bahamas, and the coastal belts of mahogany forest have been exhausted.

By the close of the eighteenth century there was an almost bewildering variety of mahogany furniture for increasing the convenience and comfort of life. In the bedroom there were light and delicately ornamental four-posters; wardrobes; bow-fronted and serpentine-fronted chests; tallboys; toilet mirrors; dressing-tables, most intricately equipped; and even washstands. In the dining-room there were sideboards, mere carving tables, or more accommodating designs equipped with drawers and cupboards, bow-fronted, elliptical, concave or serpentine-fronted. There were dumb-waiters and wine-coolers. There were magnificent dining-tables that could be extended with extra leaves to accommodate any number of guests, and a table had been invented which solved for all time that most distressing problem: the conflict that occurs between human legs and wooden ones at a dinner party. This table was supported by a column at each end which rested on four feet splayed outwards, really a revival of the principle of support used in the fifteenth- and sixteenth-century trestle tables. For seating in every part of the house chairs had developed manifold elegances and comforts. There were easy-chairs and settees and window-seats and sofas;

upholstery had become a union of decorative display with comfort. All this furniture was consistently well proportioned: it exhibited a regard for human contours. Not all of it was beautiful; but its makers never erred through ignorance of good proportion nor neglect of common sense. If ever it was a little worrying to the eye, it was because of the exuberance of its maker, who, in his anxiety to be modish, occasionally overdid his effects and became muddled.

Thomas Sheraton, although he began life as a journey-man cabinet-maker, did not practise furniture-making on the fashionable scale of his predecessors Chippendale, Hepplewhite and Shearer. No piece of furniture can be definitely attributed to him, and he is known chiefly for his influence upon contemporary design. In 1791 Sheraton published *The Cabinet Maker and Upholsterer's Drawing Book*, which went into a second edition in 1793 and a third in 1802. In 1802 and 1803 Sheraton issued another work, entitled *The Cabinet Dictionary, containing an Explanation of all the Terms used in the Cabinet, Chair and Upholstery Branches, Containing a Display of Useful Articles of Furniture*. A far more elaborate book was issued in parts in 1804 under the title of *The Cabinet Maker, Upholsterer and General Artist's Encyclopaedia*. Sheraton died in 1806, and eighty-four plates of *Designs for Household Furniture* were published six years after his death.

The conditions under which Sheraton produced his work were peculiar and unusual. It is doubtful whether he ever came into contact with any of the fashionable architects of the period. His surroundings were squalid. After he came to London in 1790 and started to write books, he apparently abandoned cabinet-making for

Design for a 'Ribband Back' chair, from *The Gentleman and Cabinet-Maker's Director*, by Thomas Chippendale (first edition, 1754). Compare with chairs on Plates XX and XXII.

107

authorship, interspersed with the delivery of sermons and the teaching of drawing. This picture of Sheraton is given in *The Memoirs of Adam Black*, for when the young Scottish founder of that publishing house first came to London he lodged with Sheraton for a few days.

There is about all Sheraton's designs an almost brittle fragility. He made drawings not only of chairs and tables and bookcases and beds, but designs for window drapery and schemes of interior decoration. He was addicted to complicated draperies, and, like Chippendale, the bed seemed to tempt him to fatuous extravagances. The glazed doors of bookcases and secretaires also enabled him to indulge in spidery complexities; queer involved glazing bars; meagre pediments, thinly upraised above the cornice line. On his sideboards and cabinets he used inlaid lines of box and ebony, shell devices and narrow curls and scrolls of ornament. He invented a number of intricate dressing-tables and washstands, also cheval glasses, work-tables and various complicated dual-purpose pieces of furniture, such as tables that could be converted into library steps, and other specimens of ingenious cabinet-making, with ingenuity often eliminating comeliness.

Sheraton designed such a variety of furniture, and bequeathed so many ideas, that his influence lasted well into the nineteenth century, although after the third decade the forms he originally set down were subjected to distortions which would have caused him considerable pain had he lived to see them. In his book there was a multiplicity of table models: sofa-tables, library-tables, work-tables, every form of writing-table. Most of his designs lacked compactness. He was so determined to be elegant at all costs; and thin legs, attenuated frames and light touches of ornament were restlessly united, often to the detriment of good proportion. Looking through pages of these lean and shrunken things, it seems as though the furniture of the late eighteenth century died in a decline, that it wasted away, became rickety. All the robust and florid curves of the mid-eighteenth century had gone. Sometimes the bold, concave or elliptical front of a sideboard would suggest the more forcible cabinet-making of the thirties and forties of the century, and often in the simpler pieces made under Sheraton's influence we may discern the respect for proportion and understanding of appropriate ornamentation which distinguished the best work of the early Chippendale type of furniture. The mahogany inlaid chest of drawers, illustrated by Fig. 68 on page 97, shows how furniture of the Sheraton type could achieve great refinement of decoration, and a reduction of material to the barest structural necessities without loss of dignity. The satinwood side-table shown in Fig. 73 on the same page comes perilously close to flimsiness. Those frail turned legs, spun to a slenderness that almost snaps; that wiry stretcher with its platform for a tiny urn; those minute ball feet: surely when this was made the English cabinet-maker had begun to abandon his traditional convictions about stability? Compare that satinwood side-table with the Adam pier-table on page 91, Fig. 66. It is only twenty years later, but by comparison the Adam table seems almost stout, and if you compare it as we compared the Adam table previously with the console table on page 83, Fig. 52, the Sheraton model becomes positively ethereal, a mere bubble of wood, scarcely able to support the weight of the balloon clock that rests upon its top.

Compare the satinwood elbow-chair with the cane-back, the satinwood settee covered in silk, and the single chair in satinwood with painted decoration on page 103 (Figs. 76, 77, 78), with the shield-back chairs and settee shown on page 87 (Figs. 63, 64, 65). The satin-wood Sheraton types are barely a quarter of a century older than the Hepplewhite shield-back types, and yet the refining influence which was begun by Adam and continued by Hepplewhite is carried so much further that we cannot help wondering whether it had not been carried too far. When Sheraton took to authorship and the drawing-board he may have parted insensibly, after a few years, with some of his disciplined reverence for material. Robert Adam knew how far delicacy of line could be practised. Many of Sheraton's designs suggest that he was incapable of judging how far slimming could be taken in the form of furniture.

The ornament which Sheraton used was nearly all classical in origin. Here and there were little touches of Egyptian decoration, a sphinx's head in place of a lion's mask. There was a short-lived Egyptian fashion in the reign of Louis XVI which may have affected English furniture-makers' ideas of ornament. England was never quite free from French influence throughout the eighteenth century. But anything that was borrowed was so skilfully adapted that foreign fashions ceased to have any major effect on English design until the first twenty years of the nineteenth century. In France at that time an elaborate and chastely classical style was established. Napoleon surrounded himself with furniture that was authentically Roman in character. This French Empire fashion hardly influenced English furniture-makers and architects. The Greek revival of the

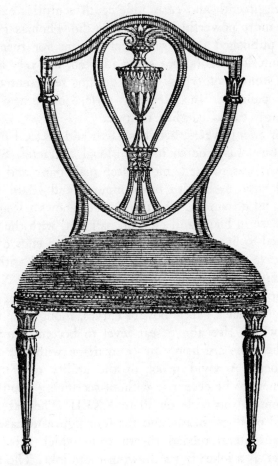

A Hepplewhite shield-back chair with a vase splat. (Compare with Figs. 63, 64 and 65, page 87.) Reproduced from *The Cabinet-Maker and Upholsterer's Guide: or a Repository of Designs for every article of Household Furniture*, by A. Hepplewhite & Co. (London, 1789). Like Chippendale's *Director* and Ince and Mayhew's *Universal System of Household Furniture*, Hepplewhite's *Guide* was a trade catalogue.

late eighteenth and early nineteenth centuries exerted
a far more powerful influence. So did Thomas Hope,
who published pseudo-classical designs for furniture
and interior decoration; some adapted, not very aptly,
from stone prototypes. These designs represented the
birth pangs of the Regency style, sometimes mis-
leadingly called English Empire.

For twenty years, between 1810 and 1830, English
furniture was true to its traditional character. Sometimes it was painted, more often mahogany and rosewood were used with brass mounts and inlaid brass
lines and ornament. The frontispiece shows a Regency
bookcase in black and gold on ball feet, with the back
stepped to fit over a dado rail. The curved ends of this
bookcase with their fluted fronts correspond with the
curving lines of chairs of this period. On Plate XXVI
a cane-seated chair with sphinx heads below the arm
terminals has a subtle flow of curves, though the front
legs which rise above seat level to become supports
for the arms are heavy by comparison with the other
members. A vivid proof of the ability of English
designers to be eccentric without sacrificing good proportions is the table on Plate XXVII. The base, su-
ported on dogs' heads, and the four figures encased in
a quadrilateral reeded sheath from which their feet
project, is a joke; but a drawing-room joke. The most
perfect propriety of form is preserved. Probably this
table was inspired by the designs of Thomas Hope.
The choice of materials and the finish demonstrate the
English furniture designer's ability to accommodate
any freak of fashion without making his work ridiculous. What later age could indulge in such fooling
without fear of vulgarity? What later age could have

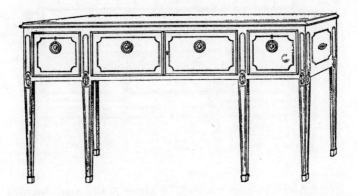

A Sheraton sideboard in mahogany, of a very simple type. It has been in the possession of Adam and Charles Black, the publishers, since the early nineteenth century, and there is a tradition that it may have been made by Sheraton for Adam Black, who lodged at Sheraton's house when he first came to London. *From a drawing by Marcelle Barton.*

produced the Pavilion at Brighton without parting with every shred of architectural decency? The Pavilion at Brighton is just such another piece of fooling as this table, although on a larger scale. Both were the work of designers to whom the principles of architectural design were vital guides.

Designers and patrons were still educated at the end of the Georgian period. Visual tranquillity was still prized. The orderly stucco streets and mansions of Nash and his contemporaries were giving a mellow dignity to London, Brighton, Hove, Cheltenham and Tenby. In that age of fine street-planning when houses still had noble proportions, furnishing was a harmonious complement to the decorative background and form was not debased by a mindless appetite for novelty.

*Above*: A rush-seated settee, made by Morris & Company, described as a 'settle' and sold for £1 : 15s. This was a moderate price for a piece of well-made, simple furniture in the eighteen-eighties.

*Right*: Sideboard designed by Philip Webb (1831–1915) and made by Morris & Company. Described as a 'small buffet', it was 5 feet long and 1 foot 4 inches deep. The design had affinities with the simple furniture made by mid-seventeenth-century craftsmen, and foreshadows the work of Ernest Gimson, Sidney Barnsley, Ambrose Heal and Gordon Russell. Both illustrations are reproduced from *Decoration and Furniture of Town Houses*, by Robert W. Edis, pages 157 and 112. (Kegan Paul, 1881.)

## CHAPTER VI

## FURNITURE DESIGN UNDER THE ROMANTIC MOVEMENT AND THE FURNITURE TRADE, 1830–1900

In Queen Victoria and her intellectual consort, Prince Albert, the Fine Arts of Great Britain have happily found protectors, who, knowing the value of elegance and refinement, in a wealthy and commercial nation, are disposed to promote their interests with a zeal proportioned to the high moral value which they undoubtedly possess. They have distinguished themselves as lovers and guides of its noblest walks and most elevated performances; the great artists both of our own and foreign nations have been made the companions of their leisure hours, and the progress of their works from the first to the finished stages, have become the subject of Royal amusement, and the source of its more elevated and permanent enjoyments.        LONDON INTERIORS: 1841

LITTLE can be said about design between 1830 and the time when William Morris began his handicraft revival. Plenty of furniture was made. Much of it was well made. The great Georgian tradition of good proportion and convenience in use faded slowly. In some places it lived on until machine production made it possible to supply the uneducated with complicated and flimsy things instead of structurally sound and relatively simple furniture. Taste either ossified in romantic antiquarianism, or else it degenerated into a snobbish appetite for lavish display.

The romantics went Gothic with a spiky profusion of pinnacles, crotchets, finials and pointed arcading. Carving came into fashion again, and sideboards, tables

115

and chairs crawled with floriated *motifs*, which were supposed to convey an authentic mediaeval air. This mode followed contemporary architecture, which was bursting into the full disorder of the Gothic revival, while John Ruskin's sonorous directions for the achievement of aesthetic anarchy encouraged everyone to despise the principles of design and the attainment of good proportion.

Everything was judged by realistic standards. Carving was realistic. Ornamental conventions were no longer appreciated, unless they were heraldic. All surfaces were crowded with decoration that did nothing to unify the design of any piece of furniture; every area was unrestfully competitive and individually self-contained. In the heavily carved furniture of early Georgian times, every leaf of acanthus, every swelling moulding, were articulate parts of a general design which was conceived as a whole. In the heavily carved furniture of early Victorian times every scrap of ornament made strident claims for attention at the expense of general unity in the design. Such gross stuff was made by craftsmen working for tradesmen, and those tradesmen supplied customers whose taste demanded realism in the execution of ornament and was complicated by a romantic love of the 'good old times'.

One of the most ardent of the Gothic revivalists, August Welby Northmore Pugin (1812–52), published designs for Gothic furniture, and provided many examples of ornament for imitation. He was perhaps the last architect to exert a distinctive influence upon furniture design generally. Possibly Sir Walter Scott was really responsible for associating Gothic forms with 'the good old times'; but this amalgam of ideas led to spurious heartiness in the decoration of furniture and a rollicking confusion of form.

All the dropsical symptoms of bad taste that had appeared under the patronage of the new rich in Elizabethan and early Stuart furniture again emerged as education was weakened by prosperity. Swollen turning destroyed the proportions of chair and table legs; squat, inflated upholstery bulged inelegantly in libraries and studies, while spidery contortions reigned in the drawing-room and boudoir. Various queer styles were invented by the furniture trade; and the most memorable of these outcrops of ingenuity was the papier-maché furniture made in the 'forties and 'fifties. This material, finished generally in black, was painted and inlaid, sometimes with ivory and mother-of-pearl; and trays, occasional-tables, work-tables, tea-tables and chairs of different types were made of it. Views of buildings or chaste landscapes sometimes formed the chief ornamental feature; and a set of papier-maché chairs might combine accommodation with moral antiquarian improvement by having pictures in colour of English cathedrals applied to their backs and protectively varnished.

The most distinctive chair made in the Victorian period was the balloon-back type, called a 'Quaker' chair when it had a rounded, upholstered seat. It had the merit of simplicity, which was cancelled out by the crime of bad proportion. In the country good, sound, simple chairs were still made; and to this day High Wycombe produces Windsor chairs in much the same forms that were used in the early nineteenth century, for the Windsor chair is a type that can be and has been intelligently adapted for mechanical production, although even now the 'bogers' or turners produce largely by hand in scores of little workshops in the Buckinghamshire woods a large proportion of the beech legs and rails of the Windsor chairs that are assembled in Wycombe factories.

The suite ruled the ideas of Victorian furniture-makers. It was the last vestige of Georgian unity, and the awful sterility of the mercantile alliance of retailer and manufacturer was demonstrated by the monotony of those mahogany chairs and tables and sideboards that proclaimed their relationship by identical assortments of bloated ornament. The provision of shelves and tables and complicated cabinets was an important activity of the furniture industry, for the Victorians accumulated minor possessions with an enthusiasm that would have been short-lived except in an age of cheap and abundant domestic labour.

Mr. Roger Fry in his essay on 'The Ottoman and the Whatnot'[1] recalls 'a genuine modern style which as yet has no name, a period of black polished wood with spidery lines of conventional flowers incised in the wood and then gilt. These things must have belonged to the 'eighties—I think they went with the bustle. . . .' By the end of the eighteen-fifties every trace of Georgian order had vanished from furniture design and from furnishing and interior decoration. William Morris and his friends had discovered after building the Red House that it was impossible to buy anything that was well designed, and in 1861 they founded Morris and Company, which was to remedy this diseased condition of decorative and applied art.[2] They did not dream of

[1] In *Vision and Design.*

[2] 'William Morris in 1859 commissioned his friend and fellow-student Philip Webb to build him a house, and in so doing he came near to inaugurate

restoring respect for Georgian order; they were infected with the Romantic movement, and their eyes sought and found in the Middle Ages what they confidently believed to be the golden age of craftsmanship. Philip Webb, Burne-Jones, Rossetti, Ford Madox Brown, Faulkner and Marshall assisted Morris to found this firm; and it started a new fashion for 'hand-made' things. The furniture trade presently began to manufacture articles that were labelled 'hand-made', with surfaces mechanically roughened or spattered with mock hammer-marks to suggest the honest toil of muscular fingers. But the example of Morris's work was to lead the furniture trade into a deeper morass of imitation, in which it flounders to this day.

There were occasional attempts to resurrect older styles of furniture in the last thirty years of the nineteenth century. Most of those artistic revolts were abortive, and the pages of *Punch* show that heavy furniture and overpowering decoration still formed the background of social life. The aspidistra upheld its leaves, a cluster of flimsy short swords, proclaiming, according to legend, the wealth of the family, for each leaf was supposed to represent a hundred pounds of the householder's annual income. Everybody collected odds and ends that were supposed to be 'artistic'. That ill-used word nearly always implied the *application* of a finish or a pattern to an object, or the introduction of an extraneous article—a piece of pottery or glass or metalwork. And the furniture trade, varying its principal activity of providing respectable masses of mahogany

a new manner. This house was to be something more than a dwelling, it was to stand as a solid declaration of faith. It was to be the architectural statement of the beliefs of the Arts and Crafts movement.'—C. and A. Williams-Ellis, *The Pleasures of Architecture*, chap. iii.

for solid and respectable English subjects, was able to make a few 'artistic' experiments in period furniture. They were sporadic experiments. It was not until the increasing power of William Morris's teaching had un-intentionally encouraged reactionary tendencies in taste that the furniture trade really felt sure of a market for 'the period styles'.

Some architects in this Victorian disorder mourned the control they had lost over design. In 1880 Mr. Robert W. Edis, F.S.A., F.R.I.B.A., delivered a series of Cantor lectures before the Society of Arts, and pub-lished them in an amplified form as a book the following year, entitled *Decoration and Furniture of Town Houses*. He had something to say about contemporary furnish-ing, and little of it was complimentary. He wrote: 'I must be forgiven if, as an architect, I regret that in these days the designing of furniture is, as a rule, handed over to the upholsterer, and that the houses we build are oft-times filled with articles incongruous in design, bad in taste, and often utterly commonplace and uncomfortable. This criticism does not apply to some of our principal manufacturers, who have striven to lead the public into more artistic thoughts, and have pro-vided for them work which is at once good in design and treatment, graceful and pleasant in form, and finished in the highest possible way, both as regards artistic character and skill of handicraft. But these gentlemen, like other artists, have a cloud of imitators, whose works are set forth as of "Old English", "Queen Anne", or some other special and equally applicable period or fashion, and which, while aiming to be cheap, are equally commonplace and nasty, and are filled with carvings of the most execrable character, or with some miserable painted daub, bad in drawing and in colour, which is made to do duty as a panel, and is set forth as high art; and from its gaudiness—or, if you like it better, eccentricity of design—commends itself to those whose taste is not of the highest kind, but whose ambition to possess gaudy finery and something to show off, is great and insatiable.'[1]

A little earlier in his book, Mr. Edis mentions a new fashion 'dedicated to her most sacred Majesty, Queen Anne, a fashion which has developed much of really good art character, and which, after all, properly applied, is really bringing us back to old English work'. He does not seem able to judge the work of any period save by its ornamentation. To him, and to his contemporaries, the character of furniture appeared to be derived from its embellishment, and not only do the illustrations in his book confirm this but it is suggested by this sentence: 'Nor is extravagance of cost necessary for the fitting up of our houses; for I hold that furniture of thoroughly good art design, comfortable in shape, and good in workmanship, may be made without any extravagant outlay, and that plain polished or painted deal furniture, of really good design, is better than all the elaboration of Chippendale fretwork or Queen Anne ornamentation'.[2]

The restless roving among the forgotten styles of the Georgian age that Victorians with some pretensions to taste indulged in during the 'eighties is inexplicable. Perhaps a sense of loss was aroused by William Morris's denunciation of contemporary design, which could not be appeased by the mediaeval solutions Morris proposed and practised. A suggestion that England at that time

[1] Pp. 34-5.   [2] P. 16.

121

was suffering from a belated rococo phase is made by Adolph Reichwein in his book *China and Europe*. It is an interesting Continental view of English taste.

'In the eighties of the nineteenth century, the appearance was noted of an "English Rococo" as a curious temporary phase of culture. This development is generally known among theorists of art as "English aestheticism". The fact that Botticelli, although he had been known long before, has since then continued to be a special favourite with the English public, is to be ultimately ascribed to a state of soul which once more preferred just these lines and just these colours rather than others. That Rossetti was admired at the time along with Botticelli, that his favourite flowers, the lily, with its soft delicate curves and slender stem, and the sunflower, were to be seen on so many tables in England —who can say why this was so? All that can be said is that people did fall in love once more with the delicate colours and graceful stems of these flowers; they fell in love, too, with the delicate hues of porcelain. Rossetti collected blue and white Chinese porcelain. And all England, by unuttered mutual consent, suddenly did the same. Need it then astonish us to learn that the old eighteenth-century furniture was once more dragged forth from dusty lumber rooms, just for the sake of its delicately curved lines? Chairs, wardrobes and elegant spider-legged tables again received the place of honour. For the furniture of Sheraton, so long dispossessed by the plain and solid Victorian furniture, every village and every cottage was ransacked. Even the furniture factories remodelled themselves on Chippendale and Sheraton.'[1]

Such a reorientation of design did not take place then

---

[1] P. 71. J. C. Powell's translation, 1925 English edition.

in the furniture trade. The passion for discovering old furniture in lumber-rooms and cottages had not yet developed into a force that was to change the economic structure of the furniture trade. The Victorian public was too devoted to extraneous fancy work, too insensitive to good proportion, to appreciate anything designed in the Georgian age. After all, Mr. Edis in 1881 could write: 'The age of Batty Langley produced furniture as false and meretricious in taste as the rooms it was designed to fill'.[1] The romantic movement had destroyed the judgement of architects; the furniture trade had destroyed the traditional common sense of designers, and machinery had almost destroyed the craftsmen.

[1] *Decoration and Furniture of Town Houses*, p. 30.

A drawing-room chair back, illustrated in the 1836 edition of George Smith's *Cabinet-Maker and Upholsterer's Guide*. Compare this top-heavy, clumsy muddle of carved ornament with the firm outlines that control the elaborate design of the 'Ribband Back' chair on page 107, and with the elegant Hepplewhite chair on page 111.

123

## CHAPTER VII

FURNITURE DESIGN UNDER THE ANTIQUE
DEALERS AND ARTIST-CRAFTSMEN, 1900–
1920

WILLIAM MORRIS believed that only by turning back to the past could civilised amenities be preserved. That industry could ever be made orderly and clean and civilised never occurred to him; and perhaps in the days when Victorian individualism was unchained and raging, any idea of tidying up industry may well have seemed quite hopeless. Outraged by its external untidiness, by its vast carelessness, by its casual pollution of water, land and air, Morris put industry out of his mind as far as he could, and never thought of its potential activities, of what it might be made to do if designers took a share in controlling it instead of leaving it entirely in the hands of business men and uncaring technicians. If William Morris had lived in these disillusioned times instead of in a period when industrial prosperity seemed so safe, so certain, so amply assured of progressive expansion, his conviction that mechanical production was evil might have impelled him to start a really vigorous movement for its abolition. Living when he did, he only founded an escapist cult, which has comforted a large number of nervous and ineffectual people ever since.

Sir Hubert Llewellyn Smith, in *The Economic Laws*

THE ANTIQUE DEALERS AND ARTIST-CRAFTSMEN

*of Art Production*, discusses the repudiation of the pro-
ductive powers of industry by William Morris. 'No
one', he writes, 'was more keenly sensible than William
Morris of the inherent contradiction between certain
features of the revival of English arts and crafts, which
he initiated, and the social and economic conditions of
the mass of the English population at the time. His own
art production, magnificent as it was, was predominantly
an *art de luxe*, and so far as its patrons were private
individuals they were mostly persons far above the
average in riches. This was certainly not because the
prices charged were excessive, but because the works
were essentially costly to produce. There is evidence in
Dr. Mackail's *Life of William Morris* that the contradiction was to him a continual source of disquiet. His
own proposed solution was not to reconcile his art work
to the necessities imposed by current conditions (that
would probably have seemed to him a debasement of
art), but rather to bring art within reach of the mass of
the people by a total change in their economic position.'[1]
To effect this change Morris wanted a revolution. To-
day we are apt to forget his militant socialism, and can
recall only the passive dreaming of *News from Nowhere*.
While awaiting the social revolution, you went to the
Cotswolds and did weaving or exotic embroidery upon
slippers, committing the most fearful patterns in the
name of handicraft, a practice deemed necessary before
the decree *nisi* of divorce from one's own century could
be pronounced. The result of all this self-conscious
withdrawal from the industrial age was the hermit
craftsman. Numbers of people retired from the world
into remote parts of the country and started to make

[1] Chap. iv, p. 122.

furniture by hand. Some of them were disciples of William Morris, some of them were just inept dabblers who were prepared to palm off any crudity in the shape of woodwork under the label of 'hand-made'. A few were artist-craftsmen of a high order, among them being such men as Ernest Gimson, Sydney Barnsley and Romney Green. A number of talented architects were at work influencing the form of modern furniture, and of these, C. F. A. Voysey (1857–1941) was the great pioneer of what is now known as the modern movement in design.

William Morris began a great revival of craftsmanship which was almost lost in the wastes of mediaeval romanticism. In England his work spawned the cult of the antique, which fostered the growth and prosperity of the most fantastically ridiculous trade that has ever existed in any country, namely, the antique furniture and faking business. Abroad, William Morris was taken far more seriously, and in Sweden his work was such a source of inspiration that the great contemporary flowering of Sweden's arts and crafts, which has enabled that talented country to produce such exquisite things in furniture, textiles, metalwork and glass, and to promote so many effective partnerships between designers and manufacturers, may be attributed in part to Morris's influence.

The modern movement in architectural design which was preached in the 'nineties and the opening decade of the present century by such men as Adolf Loos, was activated by the work of C. F. A. Voysey, and by the Scottish architect, C. R. Mackintosh (1869–1928). By many Continental architects and designers, and by our own discerning practitioners and critics of design,

Voysey is rightly regarded as the father of the modern movement. Unfortunately for this country, the modern movement did not have a clear, uninterrupted development. It became complicated by all sorts of queer and distorted foreign ideas. George Walton, who died in December 1933, another of the pioneers of modern design in England, began his v.ork in Glasgow in 1888, working among the founders of the Glasgow school of painters. In a letter to the *Architectural Review*, a few months before his death, he wrote: '... About 1892, while in Glasgow, C. R. Mackintosh followed, and our work was interesting the Dutch, and later the Austrian architects, and the type of work we were then doing would, I think, even to-day have been looked upon as modern, but unfortunately the movement, after being distorted and twisted, returned from Austria through Paris, and finished in *l'art nouveau*.'[1]

This new art was the special misfortune of original design in England. Its leering exuberance, its fantastic writhings, scared respectable people. It was hardly sobered down by the furniture trade, who borrowed its worst manifestations of ornament, misapplied them of course, and called the result the 'quaint' style. 'Quaint' indeed! Fortunately it did not survive; but it consolidated the reluctance of English people to accept new artistic experiments. The bright coiling branches and slithery leaves of new art decoration seemed so alien, so vividly ungenteel to minds respectably attuned to what were called 'furnishing colours'—crimson, dingy green, snuffy brown; so dangerously undisciplined to eyes that had previously looked upon and found good the congested but indisputably realistic floral tributes of

[1] July 1933.

127

the wallpaper and furniture-fabric manufacturers; so casually flimsy for the thickly clothed bodies whose pompous curves has hitherto been supported by the dignities of mahogany, swollen with all the pride of obese turning. Yet fluid decoration had not been unknown in England before. There were impeccable precedents for naturalistic forms: those chasing, curving vine-leaf friezes of early Tudor times; the streaming foliage of Gothic stone-work.[1] Even heart-shaped piercing is to be found in the back splats of country-made Georgian chairs occasionally.[2] But these things were forgotten; or perhaps they were never heard of by the late Victorians. People were only anxious to be relieved of the shouting, carnival vigour of this strange style. It went, and with it went all hope of encouragement or widespread patronage for original design.

Apart from experimental work by the late Sir Ambrose Heal (1872–1959), hardly anything modern was made in London in the opening of the twentieth century. Anybody who wanted furniture was on the look-out for 'bargains' in old things. There were honest and earnest attempts to recapture the 'charm' of Georgian and Stuart interiors. The word 'charm' was bandied about together with the word 'artistic' until both terms ceased to have any meaning in the English language. They have gone the way of 'quality', 'exclusive', and 'original': words that have been applied to so many

---

[1] The Romano-British period is rather remote, but there is in the Reading Museum a mosaic pavement removed from Silchester (from house No. 2 Insula XIX, excavated 1898) that foreshadows the creepy-crawly tendencies of new art. In the outer border of this pavement there are long tendrils bearing leaves, each like a curly ace of spades. It might have been shown in the Paris Exhibition of 1900 as an entirely original design.

[2] See piercing on back splat of Windsor chair on Plate XXXII.

shoddy and disreputable things by traders that they are now devoid of significance. Presently the antique dealer added 'genuine' and 'restored'.

'I want to see your reproductive furniture', said the innocent client to the salesman in a New York store. Well might it be called 'reproductive', this stuff labelled 'antique'; and *The New Yorker* when it published that joke was more apt than perhaps its editors realised. The word 'restored' only came into current use when it was beginning to be obvious that the supply of antiques was not inexhaustible, and also it enabled furniture to breed as it were, as one can read very cheerfully in *Quinneys*, so that a couple of chairs could become a set of six by parting with a leg and a stretcher, an arm and a back splat, the missing pieces being made up with new parts, and the set of six could then be described as being genuine 'pieces' of antique workmanship. There was a fortune in the word 'restored', and showroom after showroom in London and the provinces was filled and emptied month by month and year by year, and into the homes of the credulous this crippled crowd of 'restored' chairs and tables and chests thrust aside for a quarter of a century the possibility of good contemporary work being encouraged by adequate patronage.

The furniture trade, seeing that antique furniture was popular began its own lamentable career of imitation. Avid of labels, it seized upon the standard descriptions of various periods. 'Jaco' stood impartially for any watered-down machine-made copy of furniture constructed between 1600 and 1680. 'Queen Anne' was attached to anything that had cabriole legs. 'Chippendale' was the term generally applied to any furniture made of dark red wood, and in the low-grade branches of furniture production, 'Chippendale' was regarded as a colour almost exclusively. 'Sheraton' meant something thinner than 'Chippendale' in form, and a few shades lighter in colour. Anything that had rather a lot of carving or stamped composition ornament glued or nailed on to its surface and was splashed about with gold paint was called 'Louis'. The big furniture-making centres in England, High Wycombe, Shoreditch, Manchester and Barnstaple and in Scotland, Beith (in Ayrshire), were all busy turning out accurate and inaccurate copies of the period styles, and in that repellent branch of furniture production known in the trade as 'medium class goods' only caricatures were made by the factories, caricatures of noble things that English designers had once taken pride in creating.

Quite unjustly, the machine was blamed for all this. The term 'machine-made' became one of abuse. But the machine was never given a chance to do its best. It was always under the control of uneducated men. It was never under the control or even under the occasional supervision of a designer. Since 1840 or thereabouts the industrial designer has been the missing technician in British industry. William Morris, with his honest disgust for shoddiness, had turned away from machinery, and, all unconsciously, began a movement which was to delay the civilising of industry for at least half a century. The best effect of William Morris's work was his inspiration of certain young artist-craftsmen and architects like Ernest Gimson. To the work of such men as Gimson, Barnsley, A. Romney Green and, since the first world war, to Gordon Russell, we owe a big proportion of the original furniture design of the twentieth century. In the 'nineties and the Edwardian period, Mr. C. R. Ashbee was designing furniture and metalwork, also George Walton, and many architects were giving thought to the creation of furniture forms, including such designers as Mr. Baillie Scott, Mr. F. W. Troup, Mr. C. R. Mackintosh and later Sir Edwin Lutyens.

Ernest Gimson and Sydney Barnsley together gave vitality to all that was best in the ideas of William Morris. Gimson met Morris in 1884.[1] For twenty-five years Gimson lived and worked at Pinbury and Sapperton in Gloucestershire. He revived something that had been waning since the advent of machine production, namely, the ability of the craftsman to design for and with a material that he loved and understood. The chapter contributed by Mr. A. H. Powell to the Ernest Gimson Memorial Volume, condenses in one paragraph the results of that work.

'At the first glance all was of an extraordinary interest. Then one saw the beauty of the work: the substance, the development of the various woods, of the ivory, the silver, the brass, of inlays of coloured woods and shell. It was inevitable that you should find in the work now and then a humorous use of peculiar materials, an enjoyment of surprise; and for the work itself I have seen educated men and women, who might have been expected to behave differently, unable, short of actual laughter, to satisfy their delight in such a perfect union of good workmanship with happy thought.'

Gimson was a craftsman endowed with the ability of a designer. He was not just a designer who dabbled in

[1] This is the date given in the Ernest Gimson Memorial Volume. This book, entitled *Ernest Gimson, His Life and Work*, was published by Ernest Benn, Limited, London, and Basil Blackwell, Oxford, in 1924.

handicraft and knew how to employ other craftsmen. It is important to recognise his ability as a designer, for it is sometimes supposed that an accomplished craftsman is by virtue of his manual dexterity a designer. The craftsman, left to his own common sense, may devise something that is fit for its purpose, but he may over-decorate it like any savage; he may be unaware of innumerable opportunities for refining the proportions of various members; he may achieve a solid straightforwardness, a rustic simplicity, but in the absence of a continuous tradition of furniture-making to nourish his invention and provide him with guiding precedents, he must improvise, and, unless he has the selective and inventive skill of a designer, his improvisations may be discords. By mastering the craft of woodworking, Gimson, the sensitive and accomplished designer, brought to furniture-making the individual genius it had lacked since the death of Sheraton. After Sheraton there had been no great names associated with English furniture. The supply of men with ideas disciplined by a craftsman's training had dried up: there were plenty of drawing-board men, and the Victorian age is grim with the indiscretions of their taste. Sheraton was a craftsman before he started publishing books on design; Hepplewhite was a craftsman; so was Chippendale. Gimson's affinities with the traditional English craftsman are indisputable; and posterity will probably single out his name when it seeks for evidence of early twentieth-century ability in furniture design. But he did not follow the line of fashionable designers that ended with Sheraton. His work continued, unconsciously, the developments that had been suspended by the Restoration of Charles II.

He was only concerned with working by hand. He drew no help from the machine age. He felt that any compromise with mechanical production was impossible. 'Let machinery be honest', he said, 'and make its own machine-buildings and its own machine-furniture; let it make its chairs and tables of stamped aluminium if it likes: why not?'[1] So, aiming at a mastery of the traditional methods of woodworking, he gave to a largely uncaring world beautiful examples of original furniture. He made chairs with turned legs and rails and ladder-backs and spindle-backs and rush-seats, displaying his ability for apt decoration; he made cabinets and chests and sideboards in walnut and oak, with veneering of burr-elm, with inlays of holly and ebony, cherry, ivory, bone and mother-of-pearl. His chairs were of oak, ash, yew, walnut and elm. He used all the gifts of English wood, those riches of colour and marking, reviving forgotten knowledge of the decorative quality of such materials as yew and elm; employing them with an ever-widening comprehension of their flexions, of their willingness to be coaxed into comely shapes when they were wisely chosen, part by part, for the work they had to do as components of a chair or a table.

There were no classic mouldings on Gimson's furniture; no trace of an architectural heritage from the Georgian age. He eased angles with chamfers. Cupboard doors were gently raised with fielded panels. He created individual pieces of furniture. The suite, which was originally a gracious invention, spoiled by the dull wits of the Victorian furniture trade, did not inspire him.

Gimson, by studying crafts that had survived a pre-

[1] *Ernest Gimson, His Life and Work*, p. 14.

carious existence in the nineteenth century, was able to recapture the natural aptitude of the English wood-worker for appropriate ornament. Craftsmen with a tradition behind them could be trusted to use decoration wisely; such wisdom, it may be repeated, does not come from executive skill alone. To-day the only wood-work that maintains a long tradition of ornamental treatment is that used in costers' barrows and farm carts. The painting of such barrows and carts, the shaping of their structural members, with the wood nicked and rounded and the angles chamfered, illustrate pre-Georgian decorative survivals.

Sydney Barnsley was a designer and maker of furniture of the same school as Gimson. It is difficult to avoid the use of terms such as 'school' in describing the work of a number of individual designers who were solving problems and practising crafts in different parts of England during the first two decades of this century. What they achieved was virtually a new start for hand-craft in this country. The lesser men in this movement produced simple crudities which suggested the bleak forms of the American 'Mission' furniture, bare and solid wooden shapes, unsoftened by any respect for visual comfort, primitive and profoundly unimaginative. From this sort of furniture arose the 'cottage' style, which ran its course before 1914 and continued in the nineteen-twenties with certain concessions made to a desire for 'colourful' gaiety. Gimson richly developed the best that was in Morris's teaching, and ultimately his work slightly stirred the ideas of the furniture trade, for, some years after his death, several manufacturers experimented with simple oak furniture that was more sophisticated than the cottage style and which bore a traceable resemblance to some of Gimson's designs.

Gordon Russell, who began making furniture of original design after the first world war, had the same profound knowledge of wood, and the same respect and sympathy for it as Gimson. His earlier work displayed many of the characteristics of the earlier school of twentieth-century hand-craft. But Gordon Russell, unlike Gimson, made many experiments in the association of hand-craft with machine-craft, and his furniture was the product of machinery intelligently combined with hand-craft, the machine doing the job best suited to it, reserving for the hands of craftsmen those tasks that used their skill most fruitfully.

Gimson and Barnsley and other craftsmen worked outside the furniture trade. Few furniture manufacturers had ever heard their names. Experiments and research work in design have, with few exceptions, been done outside the furniture trade. The most brilliant exception was Sir Ambrose Heal. It is difficult to assess the extent of his influence on contemporary design, but there can be no question that it has been widespread and has helped to educate English taste by demonstrating the virtues of simplicity, and the attractiveness of freedom from complication both in the form of furniture and the nature of interior decoration. Early Heal designs at the beginning of the century were in the Morris tradition, indicating sometimes the impress of C. F. A. Voysey's ideas, as indeed did most of the original furniture of that time; but for fifty years Heal's designs illustrated how walnut and mahogany and oak could be used for making pieces of furniture which have the formal beauty of eighteenth-century pieces but without their architectural conventions, and without ever succumbing, as the Georgian designers sometimes did, to the blandishments of rococo ideas. (See Plate XXXVI.)

Furniture design under the artist-craftsmen of the twentieth century has preserved upon a small scale the original genius of the English woodworker.

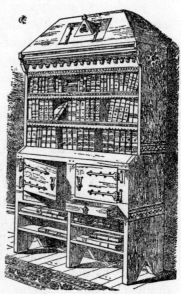

Furniture in the so-called 'Eastlake' style. *Left*: A dining-room side-board. *Right*: A library bookcase. Designed by Charles L. Eastlake, who advocated the hand polishing of wood and condemned French polishing, staining and varnishing. Both examples are from his book, *Hints on Household Taste*, a mid-Victorian best-seller. (Second edition, 1869, plates XII and XXV.)

*Above*: Design for an oak bedstead, illustrated in *The Bedroom and Boudoir*, by Lady Barker (M. A. Broome). 'Art at Home Series', Macmillan and Co., 1878. The side rails passed through the carved upright posts, and were held by wooden pins.

*Left*: An oak bedstead designed by Edgar Wood, and shown at the Arts and Crafts Exhibition, 1896. The influence of William Morris is apparent. Reproduced from *The Cabinet Maker*, November, 1896, page 115.

137

*Above*: Sideboard by George Jack, the woodwork designer for Morris & Company. Compare with the much simpler and better-proportioned design by Philip Webb on page 114.

*Right*: Folding tea-table in oak by Sidney Barnsley. Both pieces were shown at the Arts and Crafts Exhibition, 1896. From *The Cabinet Maker*, November 1896, pages 114 and 122.

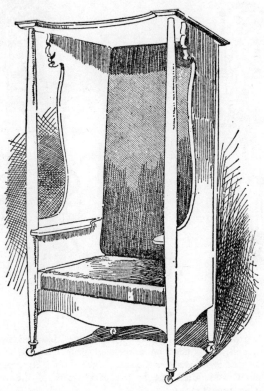

A chair by C. F. A. Voysey, shown at the Arts and Crafts Exhibition, 1896, and illustrated in *The Cabinet Maker* (November number, page 117), where it was described as a 'quaint' chair. 'In its coat and canvas of light greyish green,' said the writer, 'it seeks public favour as a new form of bedroom chair, and one can imagine how prettily it would frame up a fair invalid clad in, say, an old rose dressing-gown.' He added this reflection: 'How curiously old friends get promoted. William Morris brought the rush-seated chair from the kitchen to the drawing room. Mr. C. F. A. Voysey has carried the hall porter's chair upstairs and so purged it of its grossness that it may now be welcomed in the daintiest of bedrooms.'

A · FEW QUAINT SEATS.

*Above*: A group of seats in the 'Quaint' style, designed by Sidney Robinson, and reproduced on a reduced scale from *Furniture and Decoration and the Furniture Gazette*, 15th May 1897, plate 564. The 'Quaint' style died out in the early years of the twentieth century. (See page 127.)

*Right*: Cane-seated folding chair, from *Cassell's Household Guide*, 1875 (Volume 1, page 126). Such chairs could be bought for 17s. 6d.

*Left*: Mahogany dining-room chair, of the open balloon-back type (see page 117), leather-seated and buttoned, aggressively masculine in character. Elegance has disappeared, replaced by virile comfort. Reproduced from a trade catalogue of the eighteen-forties.

Two types of rocking chair. *Left*: Bentwood frame chair, reproduced from an advertisement by Oetzmann & Co., London, in *The Graphic*, 31st March 1883, page 331. *Right*: A 'swing' or 'platform' rocking chair, with a fixed base, by H. & A. G. Alexander & Co., of Rutherglen, near Glasgow. From *Furniture and Decoration and the Furniture Gazette*, April 1897, page 72.

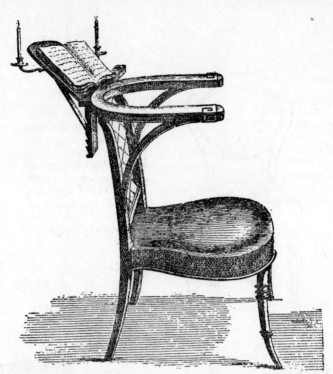

*Above*: A reading chair with an adjustable desk, included by Thomas Sheraton in his *Cabinet Maker and Upholsterer's Drawing Book* (1791–93). Like the conversation chair opposite, it was intended to encourage what Sheraton called an 'idle position'. *Below*: Victorian designers accommodated every kind of 'idle position', and this smoker's chair allowed a gentleman to lounge and smoke in comfort, without having to rise, for a drawer below the seat contained a spittoon. From *Furniture and Decoration and the Furniture Gazette*, February 1897, page 26.

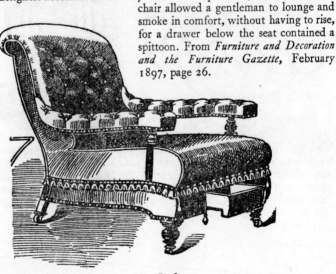

*Right*: A conversation chair, designed to allow the user to sit facing the back, while resting his elbows on the long top-rail. From *The Cabinet Dictionary*, by Thomas Sheraton, plate 29.

*Left*: 'Idle positions' of the Georgian period degenerated into undignified sprawling with the encouragement of Victorian upholsterers. From *The Adventures of Mr Verdant Green*, by Edward Bradley (Cuthbert Bede), published 1853–56, page 132.

The contrast between the Georgian and Victorian approach to design is shown by the clocks on this page and opposite. Both are related to current architectural taste, and the example above reflects the far-reaching influence of the Gothic Revival. This massive mantelpiece clock, by Edward White, of Cockspur Street, London, was shown at the International Exhibition of 1862. (Reproduced from *The Art Journal*, illustrated international catalogue, 1862, page 200.)

Case for a table clock, in the Chinese taste, by Thomas Chippendale.
The discipline of classic architecture regulates the design: the Chinese
motifs are incorporated within an orderly framework, and the Georgian
designer (unlike his Victorian counterpart) knew how to begin and
where to stop with ornament. This design, published a hundred years
before the clock on the previous page was exhibited, is reproduced
from the third edition of Chippendale's *Director* (1762), plate CLXV.

145                                                11

*Left*: Cast and wrought iron had been used for furniture and ornamental articles in the late eighteenth and early nineteenth centuries. The influence of classic design persisted. This lamp standard is reproduced from L. N. Cottingham's *Smith and Founders Director* (1823), plate XLV. Cottingham's copy-book was reprinted many times and kept alive the classic tradition. *Below*: Chair frame of cast and wrought iron, to take a wood seat; and a 'Gothic' chair, cast in three pieces and riveted together. From *The Encyclopaedia of Cottage, Farm and Villa Architecture and Furniture*, by John Claudius Loudon (1833).

By the mid-Victorian period the use of metal for chairs suggested elegant possibilities; an original style was evolving, almost by accident, and certainly without recognition as a serious contribution to furnishing. *Left*: An easy chair with a frame of flat metal strips, and a continuous upholstered back and seat, shown by Sedley of Regent Street, a London upholsterer, at the International Exhibition of 1862. (From *The Art Journal*, illustrated international catalogue.)

*Right*: Chair with wire-mesh back and seat, and slender iron frame. A type used extensively in gardens and parks. Reproduced from a drawing in *Judy*, 19th August 1868.

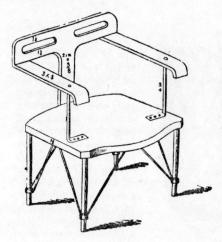

*Left*: Design for an iron elbow kitchen chair, by Robert Mallet. 'The back and elbows are cast in one piece; the supports for the elbows and also the legs are of gas tubing, screwed into a cross frame of iron, which proceeds from the back of the chair under the wooden seat.' Loudon's *Encyclopaedia* (1833).

*Right*: A Coalbrookdale garden chair in cast-iron. Firm, orderly lines give coherence to its decorative character. It may have been influenced by the work of William Morris, and the ornamental forms resemble those produced by Walter Crane and his imitators. *Drawn by Marcelle Barton and reproduced by courtesy of the British Cast Iron Research Association.*

148

## CHAPTER VIII

# THE NEW MATERIALS AND THEIR EFFECT
## ON DESIGN

NO age has a monopoly of good or bad taste. We are still slowly emerging from a period of bad taste, when original ideas were numbed or smothered. Because copyism flourished under the rule of the antique dealers, the character of contemporary materials was disregarded. Nearly every other age has thankfully used good materials, when they came to hand. Walnut was welcomed. Mahogany was welcomed and immediately employed. Upholsterers triumphantly adopted every material, device and trick of padding, stuffing and springing that could make upholstered furniture more and more comfortable. But for the first quarter of this century we accepted almost without enquiry, and with a depressing unadventurousness, the materials that had been used for the previous three centuries without trying any of the bold experiments that were possible, and which have since been tried. Chromium-plated tubular steel chairs, once supposed to represent the last word in modernism, recalled an old structural principle. John Claudius Loudon, in his *Encyclopaedia of Cottage, Farm and Villa Architecture and Furniture*, first published in 1833, showed chairs with legs of gas tubing and elbows and back cast from iron in one piece. In the sixties and seventies of the last century chairs

149

of metal rods or laminated metal strips, with X-shaped under-frames, had backs and seats of wire netting, which allowed frock-coated gentlemen and frilly ladies to recline upon an open fabric, supported by ductile frames. (See page 147.)

Victorian manufacturers made cage-like bedsteads of brass and enamelled iron rods, garnished with knobs and bosses and debased renderings of acanthus ornament. Not that metal beds and chairs represented a new idea at all, or metal furniture for that matter. The Naples Museum contains many examples of bronze furniture removed from Pompeii and Herculaneum, and in the late eighteenth and early nineteenth centuries, faithful reproductions of such furniture were cast in bronze and iron.

The distinctive character of 'modern' furniture in the late nineteen-twenties and 'thirties arose from the way designers used metal and glass and laminated wood with a rather bleak logic. Their work demanded not only a readjustment of conventional taste, but the abandonment of accepted beliefs of what it is possible to support. In *South Wind* Norman Douglas described the excavation of pumice-stone, and one of his characters commented on the spectacle of men and boys carrying huge masses of this featherweight material. 'Light as foam. But who can believe it? The bearers move within a few feet of us, and yet it resembles the most ponderous limestone or granite. . . . To me, who know the capacity of human bone and muscle, these men are a daily miracle. They mock my notions of what is permissible. How hard it is, sometimes, to trust the evidence of one's senses! How reluctantly the mind consents to reality!'

That feeling of outraged scale was induced by the tubular steel chair when it supported the bulk of a sixteen-stone man. New materials for furniture-making or a new and unsuspected use of familiar materials are inclined to disturb our sense of structural propriety. The structural revolution in furniture may be traced back to an architectural source, to Paxton's Crystal Palace, one of the first modern buildings in Europe, which began a structural revolution in architecture. The effects were reflected, as architectural influence is always reflected, in many other fields of design, and particularly in furniture. The structural revolution in architecture has destroyed the importance of the wall. Buildings used to be like crustaceans, with a hard external supporting shell. The wall was strong and thick and upheld the floors and roof. Now buildings have changed into vertebrates; they have a staunch internal skeleton of steel, and the walls support nothing, but clothe the steel skeleton like a skin. The patrons of architecture during the first half of this century seldom recognised the fact of this revolution or acknowledged its aesthetic consequences. In furniture we copied antique models. In building we veneered the front of steel skeletons with costly, pseudo-classical or even Assyrian stone façades.

At the beginning of the century the new art movement produced some abortive experiments in metal furniture. It was all drawing-board stuff, unrelated to the material, and its sinuous, floreated lines could have been expressed equally well in butter. Except for such starkly utilitarian articles as filing cabinets and other office equipment, there were few serious attempts to create metal furniture until this branch of design was revived by the 'modern movement' after the 1914–18 War. Germany, released from the taste of William II, who liked corpulent carving, began to lead Europe in clean, vigorous design. (That was before design in Germany had been given political significance by a reactionary psychopath and the 'art of the left' was persecuted.) Dramatic possibilities in metal were then discovered. Nickelled and chromium-plated steel and polished aluminium came into alliance with yielding upholstery of leather and rubber, and chairs and couches appeared, strictly metallic in character, as efficient as sanitary fittings, and, at first, just about as interesting. The crude ruthlessness of such beginnings was gradually modified; tubular metal furniture became more civilised, less insistent upon stark lines: its designers made some acknowledgement to humanity.

Although the furniture-maker was no longer directed by the influence of the architect, as he had been in the eighteenth century, the architect ultimately controls the form, size, capacity and character of all furniture, for he provides the accommodation for it, admits or denies the necessity for its existence. In the efficiently equipped rooms of modern houses and flats, the fitted cupboard has replaced the large wardrobe and competent plumbing has replaced the washstand.

The type of architectural design arising from the structural revolution has stimulated the invention of furniture designers who have emptied their minds of traditional prejudices. The process of emptying the mind of traditional prejudices does not imply that appreciation for the subtleties of proportion has to be jettisoned. 'Proportion is a due adjustment of the size of the different parts to each other and to the whole; on this proper adjustment symmetry depends.' Thus, Marcus Vitruvius Pollio in the third book of his work on architecture. This piece of wisdom is not a limiting law; it is an activating principle. A modern building of steel and concrete, aluminium, plastics and glass can achieve nobility of proportion. Furniture designers and the furniture industry have now accepted contemporary materials, finding new uses also for traditional materials. For example, glass for two and a half centuries had been employed simply for windows or mirrors. Cabinets and bookcases and bureau-bookcases had glass fronts, small panes set in wooden glazing bars. In the nineteenth century the mirror-fronted wardrobe was invented, and glass acted as a protective covering for some fine piece of wood. Often an antique dining-table would remind its possessors that it was almost a museum-piece, by having a plate glass top to preserve its figuring and patina from the coarse contacts incidental to everyday use. That glass could be used as an independent material was seldom recognised, until new properties removed it from the class of fragile materials. Toughened glass and strong polished plate glass began to be used in conjunction with frames of steel or light alloys. Then, after the second world war, the plastics industry, greatly expanded by wartime needs and enriched by many fresh processes, released another branch of industrially produced materials as a challenge to furniture manufacturers and designers.

Hitherto, the history of English furniture had been the history of woodworking, of advances in skill, of the introduction of new woods, new tools, new techniques,

153

new forms of ornament and decoration. Now the maker and the industrial designer were given a remarkable range of malleable and ductile materials: plastics, which were capable of being moulded under heat and pressure; aluminium and its alloys; plywood and laminated board; wood and linen and paper impregnated with resin; and many new forms of glass. This great range of materials had a revolutionary effect on design; vastly different from changing, say, from walnut to mahogany, or from mahogany to rosewood; the furniture trade was no longer wood-bound, though a decade passed before the full meaning of such liberation was understood. The new materials, produced by industrial processes, could only be economically fabricated by industrial methods; and this seemed to exclude the craftsman as completely as he had been excluded in the early days of mechanical production, but his successor, the industrial designer, had infiltrated the furniture manufacturing trade, and had realised the value of the research work in design and materials carried out by the artist-craftsmen of the nineteen-twenties and 'thirties, the men who had used machinery instead of rejecting it, like the artist-craftsmen of the Morris school. Already the lineaments of what we now call 'contemporary' furniture had been discernible in much of the hand-made furniture, designed by men like Sir Ambrose Heal and Sir Gordon Russell. (See Plates XXXVI, XXXVII and XXXIX.) All the robust attributes of the handicraft revival inspired their work; but they understood the technique of mechanical production; they never worked in isolation from machinery, as Gimson had worked.

Designers who have such understanding select and

handle materials with the same sympathy and mastery
exhibited by the joiners and carpenters, turners, cabinet
makers and carvers, who used wood in the seventeenth
and eighteenth centuries. They achieve and maintain a
comparable mastery of steel and light alloys, plywood,
plastics and glass. The late Percy Smith went to the
root of the matter when he once said: 'I would suggest
that it is quality of design, even more than quality of
material, which gives sustained value and interest.
Bronze, for instance, is a noble material, but if something made of bronze is poorly designed it is boring
instead of stimulating, and is soon neglected, or used
merely as a convenience and only until something
better is produced. The same principle applies to
plastics. It is qualities of style and of design which
confer reasonably sustained satisfaction.'[1]

The 'qualities of style and design' are derived only
from the trained imagination of a designer, who becomes familiar with the materials of his own age, and
the mechanical methods for fabricating them. 'Economy is a virtue proper to machinery,' observed Gordon
Logie in *Furniture from Machines*, 'but there is a great
difference between the economy that results from clean
design and efficient production, and that produced by
shoddy materials and scamped construction and finish.'[2]

This is exactly the sort of honesty in design that
Gimson meant in his remark about machine-made
furniture quoted on page 133. 'Machines used intelligently', Logie contends, 'can produce furniture of

[1] *Contribution to a discussion on* The Influence of Plastics on Design, *by
Percy Smith, R.D.I. Journal of the Royal Society of Arts*, Vol. XCI, No. 4644,
page 470.
[2] *Furniture from Machines*, by Gordon Logie, A.R.I.B.A. (London:
George Allen & Unwin Ltd., 1947.) Preface, page ix.

excellent quality more cheaply than furniture made by hand. The furniture will not be the same as hand-made furniture. No machine can produce the delicacy and sensitivity of hand craftsmanship. What machines can do is to give us an altogether different kind of excellence.' An excellence that we may often discover in the contemporary designs of the nineteen-sixties.

The influence of architectural design has exerted an increasing influence on the form and character of furniture since the 1939–45 War. Architects are often gifted industrial designers, and their training and habitual interest in materials have often injected fresh ideas into furniture manufacturing, when manufacturers have had the wisdom to consult them. Architects like R. D. Russell (the brother of Sir Gordon Russell), Christian Barman, Brian O'Rorke, Sir Frederick Gibberd, Edward D. Mills, Sir Hugh and Lady Casson, Maxwell Fry, Jane Drew and the late Wells Coates (1895–1958), and industrial designers like A. B. Read, Misha Black and the late Ernest Race—to name only a few—have mastered and used industrial techniques. The industrial designer, then, is perhaps the logical successor to the artist-craftsman; though the craftsman is not inevitably doomed. He is unlikely to become extinct, for the desire to fashion things by hand is as old as humanity and the horrors of Aldous Huxley's *Brave New World* could only follow the reorganisation of human nature which he predicted. We still ask more from at least some of our possessions than the transitory excellence that well-designed machine-made furniture can now provide. Very little of such 'contemporary' furniture is likely to be enriched by the passage of time; those surfaces of plastic or chemically-treated wood cannot acquire the patina that age confers on oak and walnut and mahogany; and, structurally, it has everything to lose and nothing to gain from age. Examples may be preserved as objects of historical interest in some museums of the future, but are unlikely to figure in sale rooms as desirable 'antiques'. Like contemporary office buildings and passenger liners, much of the furniture made to-day has an 'economic' life. It is not designed or intended for posterity, and in this and other ways perfectly expresses the character of the scientific industrial age.

## CHAPTER IX

## THE PATIENT ART OF BUYING FURNITURE

PATIENCE is the chief requirement of those who want to buy furniture. If you want genuine old furniture, don't imagine that a few superficial tips about the location of worm-holes will protect you from the gangsters of the antique racket. Worm-eaten wood is often used for patching up some crippled chair or table, for that label 'restored' can cover practically anything—even a bureau-bookcase built around a single hinge of antique origin. It is as well to be suspicious, if not bleakly incredulous, when, after being assured that a piece of furniture is 'genuine', you can see the channelling of the galleries made by the larvae of the furniture beetle exposed on the surface of the article. That beetle burrows into wood, and its entrances and exits are indicated by little pinprick holes, and if the wood is badly attacked those holes will emit fine dust when tapped. Only when worm-eaten wood is cut are the internal galleries revealed.

If you have an affection for the shape of things designed in the past, then you should do your buying in the light of your knowledge of design. You will then discover that the 'red-hot fake' is seldom a thing of simple beauty and clean line. It is deliberately *odd*; rare only because it is eccentric; its deceit is overdone; it is intended to cheat a collector rather than to delight a connoisseur of design. It will frequently be described with a cynicism that is perhaps unintentional as a 'collector's piece'.

Before the 1914–18 War, and in the 'twenties and 'thirties, antique furniture of the country-made type was often cheaper to buy than contemporary furniture; while large, ornate pieces were practically unsaleable because they were too big for modern rooms. They still languish in hundreds of showrooms. Antique furniture of almost any kind has appreciated in value, and none of it is cheap. Early and mid-Victorian pieces are now qualified antiques. The sources of supply are unchanged.

Beware of ye olde shoppes in cathedral cities: the fakes that lurk below the clusters of warming-pans are anything from 50 to 250 per cent dearer than in London, while the genuine antiques, such as they are, are usually overpriced. The last hope of the bargain-hunter still lies in suburban second-hand furniture shops, where odd pieces of old furniture sometimes turn up and are sold at the prices asked for the normal rubbish that litters such places. If you are a casual purchaser of old furniture, or furniture of antique design, and avoid the blinding emotionalism of an avid collector, your self-esteem may remain unwounded for years, though it may suffer if and when you indulge in the pleasures of modern furnishing. You may even detect a faint flavour of the grave about your treasures then. If they are old, you are not really their owner: they are owning you—for a time. So buy some contemporary work to rub shoulders with them. There is far more contemporary furniture of good design in the nineteen-sixties than there was in the nineteen-thirties.

Unless you own enormous rooms and can reproduce therein, with or without antique designs, the dignities of furnishing in the grand manner, you may make the best of both possible worlds with old and new. Things of good design seldom quarrel with each other, no matter how far apart they are in time.

The prices of old furniture fluctuate so greatly, that any attempt to discuss costs must be hedged about with so many reservations, and little practical guidance in this difficult and disappointing matter can be given. When you begin to buy modern furniture you will need even greater reserves of patience than when the dealers are telling you the old, old story. At least the dealers know something about furniture, and the meaning of style and character. Formerly, the average retail furnisher, or head of the furniture section of a big departmental store, was not even passively ignorant of design; he was aggressively ignorant. He would claim that he knew what the public wanted. His lack of education and taste often obstructed experiments that furniture manufacturers wanted to make. Not that they made nearly enough, though the trade is now far more enterprising and enlightened than it was in the nineteen-thirties.

When buying furniture, antique or 'contemporary', sharpen your critical faculties. Cultivate sales resistance. Remember that in normal times when there is no shortage of anything in shops except good manners and efficiency, the customer is always right. It's a consumers' world. Enjoy it.

The retailer often regards you not as a customer, a person to be served and studied, but as a sales outlet, an empty space into which *stock can be shifted*. He has even fallen for the fashionable marketing jargon, and refers to the purchase of goods as 'consumer offtake'. And when jargon depletes a trader's stock of common sense, you should beware of him, because he has lost his human likeness and no longer thinks of his customers as people, as men and women with minds and souls and variegated personal taste, but as 'consuming offtakers'. He has often more junk to get rid of than the antique dealer.

Remember all the time what is happening behind the scenes. The chiefs of the retail establishments order their departmental buyers to buy what they think will sell. But even this prudent mandate is rather a gamble. The Englishman's house is still his castle, and he and his wife have queer streaks of individual adventurousness about the things they may put into it, plus an abundance of passionate obstinacy, thus rendering any mortal forecast of their purchasing inclinations impossible. The trade buyer used to fill acres and acres of deep-carpeted showrooms with 'Jaco' suites, and pseudo-Chippendale, pseudo-Adam and pseudo-Sheraton. Now he includes a high proportion of so-called 'contemporary' furniture: much of it elegant and graceful: some of it bleak and unimaginative. He doesn't like experiments which may affect departmental profits, and the most sinister figure in modern industry, the accountant, is always cracking the whip in the background, and muttering: 'Figures must be kept up!' The accountant, whose proper function is measurement not management, can murder enterprise.

'Safety first!' used to be the cry of the little old-fashioned Napoleons of commerce. 'We must make sure of the bread-and-butter stuff, gentlemen—it is hardly

practical to discuss ideals at this meeting.' And progress was carried unanimously from the board room.
A younger and on the whole more adventurous generation has replaced the nervous simpletons who did so
much to perpetuate bad design between the wars. As
we have seen, the capable designer in wood and metal
and pottery was tempted under such conditions to
become a solitary craftsman, working out his own
salvation (or bankruptcy) and inevitably losing touch
with the life and needs of his own time. He went to the
Cotswolds or the Chilterns or the Sussex Downs, and
became so deeply concerned with making things that
he forgot all about selling them. There were only
limited outlets for his work.

During the first third of the century, the artist-
craftsman either became a disgruntled hermit relying
on the chance patronage of the discriminating rich, or
else he tried, perhaps in company with other craftsmen,
to organise his work, to form a guild or a craft colony.
This was generally unsuccessful, because the organisers
were inclined to pride themselves on their ignorance of
business, ignoring such matters as costing, so that the
selling price of the things they made was sometimes
below the production cost, and sometimes so far in
advance of the manifest worth of the goods that nobody
could afford to buy them. This made the buying of
individual hand-made modern furniture as great a
gamble as bargain-hunting for antiques.

In the interval between the world wars, you had to
search, often in vain, in the wilderness of the average
retailer's showrooms for tolerable furniture. But since
the nineteen-forties well-made furniture of good design
is not so difficult to find. Contemporary furniture,

relatively simple in design, is well made and visibly well made. With traditional forms the possibilities of concealing defects and mistakes and shoddy economies are enlarged. So investigate all joints. Ornament applied to the surface of a cabinet or wardrobe or bookcase may hide careless construction. Avoid applied ornament, which often expresses the taste of the furniture manufacturer trying to please the retail buyer and is generally unspeakable.

Look all round a piece of furniture, and underneath and on top of it too. Look particularly at the backs and tops of wardrobes. Don't worry if you see plywood used for the backs of chests and wardrobes. It is a good, light material; but it must be properly used: not tacked on to the frame with unprotected edges. If there are little wedges of paper or wood underneath the feet of any piece of furniture, look the salesman in the eye and ask why they are there. You may then learn that the showroom floor is uneven, just at that place; so have the piece moved to an even place and see if it still rocks on its feet.

See that every drawer runs easily, and that cupboard doors swing shut. Take each drawer out, look underneath it, and see that the angle jointing is not slipshod and clumsy. Refuse to have anything to do with tables and chairs with legs unduly thin or fat: such deformities are produced by the inept use of woodworking machinery.

There are now many excellent and completely reliable retail furnishers. Forty years of consistent educational propaganda about good design have been effective. There is more good work to choose from; and reliable information about contemporary furniture designers and where their work may be seen and bought, is available from the Council of Industrial Design, which was founded in 1946.

Furniture design has progressively improved since the nineteen-thirties, when this book was first published. The war-time 'utility' period acted as a purge for extravagance and folly in design, comparable with the puritan regime which England suffered in the mid-seventeenth century.

CHAPTER X

## BOOKS ABOUT FURNITURE AND DESIGN

IF you have read as far as this chapter and still feel
that you *must* collect antique furniture and would
like to study the history of English furniture design in
greater detail, then many books have been published
that may improve your knowledge; but books can
never bring the familiarity with materials and construction and the intimate understanding of design which
follows the scrutiny and handling of actual pieces of
furniture. In museums and the great houses that are
open to the public, the handling of exhibits is forbidden,
though permission is sometimes granted to students.
The most practical advice to the private collector is
given by Anthony Bird, who says: 'By far the best way
to pick up information is by cultivating some friendly
and well-informed dealers, making purchases from
them when the right opportunity offers, and keeping
one's eyes and ears on the stretch in antique shops and
auction-rooms.' As a reliable guide to the history,
character and purchase of antiques, his book is placed
first in the list that follows. For a general study of the
subject, then, *English Furniture for the Private Collector*,
by Anthony Bird (B. T. Batsford Ltd., 1961), is recom-
mended, also *Old English Furniture for the Small Collector*, by J. P. Blake and A. E. Reveirs-Hopkins
(B. T. Batsford Ltd., third edition, 1948); and another

excellent survey, which includes French as well as English periods, is *Furniture: An Explanatory History*, by David Reeves (Faber and Faber Ltd., 1957). A detailed account of collectors and collecting, sumptuously produced and illustrated, was written by the late Robert Wemyss Symonds, whose untimely death occurred in 1958. He was an architect, a furniture designer, and had for many years been acknowledged as the highest authority and writer on English furniture. This book, the last to be completed during his lifetime, was entitled *Furniture Making in Seventeenth and Eighteenth Century England*, and he described it as 'An Outline for Collectors' (*The Connoisseur*, 1955).

For identification and dating, the *Dictionary of English Furniture* should be consulted. A new revised and enlarged edition by Ralph Edwards was published in 1954 in three magnificently illustrated volumes, embracing all periods from late mediaeval to late Georgian (Country Life Ltd.). A compact, though less comprehensive, work is the author's *Short Dictionary of Furniture*, which contains over 2600 terms used in Britain and America (George Allen and Unwin Ltd., 1952. Revised and enlarged edition, 1969.)

The earliest book on antique furniture, that may well have expanded the growing taste for collecting, was *Specimens of Ancient Furniture*, published in 1836 (London: William Pickering). The plates were engraved from drawings by Henry Shaw, a conscientious and accurate draughtsman, with descriptions by Sir Samuel Rush Meyrick. Though some of the pieces illustrated were spurious and faked-up, as a pioneer work the book was fairly reliable. (One of Shaw's illustrations is reproduced on page 36 of this book.)

The first work that accurately described and illustrated the principal periods was *A History of English Furniture*, by Percy Macquoid, published in four volumes separately entitled *The Age of Oak*, *The Age of Walnut*, *The Age of Mahogany* and *The Age of Satinwood* (Lawrence and Bullen, 1904–08). The classification, while superficially convenient, is ambiguous, for no period of furniture-making was exclusively identified with one particular material. There is nothing equivocal about the periods covered by the *Catalogue of English Furniture*, published by the Victoria and Albert Museum. Each of the four volumes deals specifically with an historical period: I, *Gothic and Early Tudor*, and II, *Late Tudor and Early Stuart*, by H. Clifford Smith; III, *Late Stuart to Queen Anne*, by Oliver Brackett; and IV, *Georgian Furniture*, by Ralph Edwards.

The books on furniture published during the eighteenth and early nineteenth centuries were nearly all trade catalogues, issued by cabinet-makers, upholsterers, chair-makers, carvers and gilders. (The exception was Thomas Hope's book of designs.) They were addressed to the nobility and gentry as potential customers, or to the furniture trade. The best known are included in the following list:

CHIPPENDALE, THOMAS. *The Gentleman and Cabinet Maker's Director* (1754). Third edition with additional plates, 1762.
DARLY, M. *A New Book of Chinese, Gothic and Modern Chairs* (1751).
HEPPLEWHITE, A., & Co. *The Cabinet Maker and Upholsterer's Guide, or Repository of Designs for Every Article of Household Furniture* (1788).
HOPE, THOMAS. *Household Furniture and Interior Decoration Executed from Designs by Thomas Hope* (1807).

INCE, WILLIAM, and MAYHEW, JOHN. *The Universal System of Household Furniture: Consisting of above 300 Designs in the most Elegant Taste, both Useful and Ornamental* (1759–62. First published in parts).

London Society of Cabinet-Makers. *The Cabinet-Makers' London Book of Prices* (1788).

MANWARING, ROBERT. *The Cabinet and Chair-Maker's Real Friend and Companion; or the Whole System of Chair-Making made Plain and Easy* (1765).

MANWARING, ROBERT, and others. *The Chair-Maker's Guide* (1766).

SHEARER, T. *Designs for Household Furniture* (1788).

SHERATON, THOMAS. *The Cabinet Maker and Upholsterer's Drawing Book* (1791–93. Originally published in parts).
*The Cabinet Dictionary* (1803).

SMITH, GEORGE. *A Collection of Designs for Household Furniture and Interior Decoration* (1808).
*Cabinet-Makers' and Upholsterers' Guide, Drawing Book, and Repository of New and Original Designs for Household Furniture* (1826).

Society of Upholsterers, Cabinet-Makers, etc. *Household Furniture in Genteel Taste for the Year 1760.*

Reprints of plates from the works of Chippendale, Hepplewhite and Sheraton have been reissued in a smaller and more convenient format than the originals, and of these the most notable are:

*The Furniture Designs of Thomas Chippendale: a selection of plates from Chippendale's Director,* arranged by J. Munro Bell with an introduction by Arthur Hayden (Gibbings and Co., 1910).

*Chippendale Furniture Designs, from the Director* (1762 edition), with a preface and descriptive notes by R. W. Symonds (Alec Tiranti Ltd., 1948).

*The Ornamental Designs of Chippendale, from the Director* (1762 edition), with a preface by R. W. Symonds (Alec Tiranti Ltd., 1949).

*Hepplewhite Furniture Designs, from the Guide* (1794 edition), with a preface by Ralph Edwards (Alec Tiranti Ltd., 1947).

*Sheraton Furniture Designs, from the Cabinet Maker and Upholsterer's Drawing Book* (1791–94), with a preface by Ralph Edwards (John Tiranti, 1946).

The extent of the furniture trade in the capital between 1660 and 1840 was recorded by the late Sir Ambrose Heal, who included over 2200 names in his *London Furniture Makers* (B. T. Batsford Ltd., 1953). Sheraton listed 253 'Master Cabinet-Makers, Upholsterers, and Chair-Makers, in and about London' in *The Cabinet Dictionary* (1803).

Innumerable books devoted to specific types of furniture or periods of design have been published during the present century, and the following are informative and well illustrated:

*Ancient Coffers and Cupboards* (Methuen and Co., 1902); *Old Oak Furniture* (Methuen and Co., 1905); and *Ancient Church Chests and Chairs* (B. T. Batsford Ltd., 1929), by Fred Roe.

*Old English Walnut and Lacquer Furniture* (Herbert Jenkins, 1922); *English Furniture from Charles II to George II* (The Connoisseur Ltd., 1929); *Masterpieces of English Furniture and Clocks* (B. T. Batsford Ltd., 1940); and *Veneered Walnut Furniture, 1660–1760* (John Tiranti, 1946), by R. W. Symonds.

*English Furniture of the Cabriole Period*, by H. A. Tipping (Jonathan Cape, 1922).

*English Furniture and Furniture Makers of the Eighteenth Century*, by R. S. Clouston (Hurst and Blackett Ltd., 1906).

*English Furniture: The Georgian Period (1750–1830)*, by Margaret Jourdain and F. Rose. *English Furniture and Decoration during the Later Eighteenth Century, 1760–1803* (B. T. Batsford Ltd., 1922); and *Regency Furniture* (Country Life Ltd., 1948), by Margaret Jourdain.

*English Cottage Furniture*, by F. Gordon Roe, F.S.A. (Phoenix House Ltd., 1949).

*The Craftsman in Wood*, by Edward H. Pinto, F.S.A. (G. Bell & Sons Ltd., 1962. Reprinted, 1965.)

During the first half of this century few books about the history of English furniture went beyond 1830: authors regarded the Victorian period as the dead end of good design, despite the persistence of a classic tradition that survived until the eighteen-sixties. No study of the fluctuations and peculiarities of Victorian fashions in furnishing and decoration is complete without reference to *Punch*, which was first published on 17th July 1841, and provides an authentic social history of the period. A well-documented work, *Victorian Furniture*, by R. W. Symonds, was completed after his death by his collaborator, B. B. Whineray (Country Life Ltd., 1962). A shorter but most informative book with the same title, *Victorian Furniture*, written by F. Gordon Roe, was published ten years earlier (Phoenix House Ltd., 1952). A social history of design, 1830 to 1900, entitled *Victorian Comfort*, by the author, includes chapters on furnishing (A. and C. Black Ltd., 1961). A preview of the Victorian period was given by John Claudius Loudon, in his *Encyclopaedia of Cottage, Farm and Villa Architecture and Furniture* (1833), which remained a standard copy book, long after Loudon's death in 1843. His influence on furniture design is described in *Mr. Loudon's England*, by the author (Oriel Press, 1970).

The impact of the handicraft revival was recorded in such contemporary works as Charles L. Eastlake's *Hints on Household Taste in Furniture and Upholstery* (Longmans, Green and Co., published originally in the eighteen-sixties and reaching a fourth edition in 1878); and *Decoration and Furniture of Town Houses*, by Robert W. Edis (Kegan Paul and Co., 1881). The work of the artist-craftsmen who were inspired by William Morris was periodically illustrated in the early years of this century by *The Studio*, and many examples are included in the *Studio Year Books*.

Examples of the work of the greatest of those craftsmen were collected in a memorial volume, *Ernest Gimson: His Life and Work*, published in 1924, five years after Gimson's death. (London: Ernest Benn Ltd.; Oxford: Basil Blackwell.)

Architectural and industrial design are affiliated, and the character of furniture has always been influenced by architecture. *A History of the English House, from Primitive Times to the Victorian Period*, by Nathaniel Lloyd, describes and illustrates the architectural setting for English furniture (The Architectural Press, 1931). For a wider study of architecture and the ancillary arts, the standard work is *A History of Architecture on the Comparative Method*, by Sir Banister Fletcher. (The seventeenth edition, revised by the late Professor R. A. Cordingly. University of London: Athlone Press, 1961.) Two books which repay attention are *Art and the Nature of Architecture*, by Bruce Allsopp (Sir Isaac Pitman and Sons Ltd., 1952), and *A General History of Architecture*, by the same author (Pitman, new edition, 1962). *The Architecture of England, from Norman Times to the Present Day*, by Sir Frederick Gibberd, relates architecture to other branches of design, and is a pictorial history with a running commentary. (The Architectural Press: first published 1938, and many times reprinted.) The reciprocal development of architecture and industrial design from the Middle Ages to the twentieth century is described in *The English Tradition in Design*, by the present author, who has written a companion volume, *The English Tradition in Architecture*, which begins with Romano-British building and ends with the new Coventry Cathedral (A. and C. Black Ltd., 1959 and 1963).

A broad view of the pervasive powers of national character in all branches of art is given in Sir Nikolaus Pevsner's study, *The Englishness of English Art*, an expanded and annotated version of the Reith lectures that he broadcast in 1955. (The Architectural Press, 1956.)

Industrial design is a subject that has been consciously identified and written about for barely forty years; but in that time it has fomented innumerable and very lively disputes and discussions, which generated a wide and growing interest, sustained by books and articles and exhibitions. Of those books, the most significant is the late Sir Herbert Read's *Art and Industry*, first published in 1934 (Faber and Faber Ltd.), and since reissued. Furniture comes into Sir Nikolaus Pevsner's survey, published in 1937 under the title of *An Enquiry into Industrial Art in England* (Cambridge University Press); the opening section of Michael Farr's *Design in British Industry* is concerned with furniture (Cambridge University Press, 1955), and furniture manufacturing is included in the writer's *Industrial Art Explained* (George Allen and Unwin Ltd. Revised and enlarged edition, 1946). The effect on design of contemporary materials and production techniques is described and illustrated in *Furniture from Machines*, by Gordon Logie (George Allen and Unwin Ltd., 1947) and in *The Technique of Furniture Making*, by Ernest Joyce (B. T. Batsford Ltd, 1970). An acute and original study of this branch of the subject has been made by Professor David Pye, entitled *The Nature and Art of Workmanship* (Cambridge University Press, 1968).

Year by year *The Architectural Review* and *Design*

(the monthly magazine of the Council of Industrial Design) illustrate the development and variations of the light, graceful and often elegant furniture that is now called 'contemporary', though in the twenty-first century it may well be known as 'New Elizabethan'.

Whenever people have understood the art of living, they have left behind them graceful things—furniture of intrinsic dignity, and a quiet pattern of beauty in the surroundings they created. We cannot hide our lives or any of our ways from our descendants, however far they may be separated from us by time, and however barbarous or affluent have been the gaps between their day and ours. The true image of history is revealed by the things men have made and used. Our furniture, about which dealers, designers, salesmen, craftsmen and critics have in their various ways told the tale, will tell the tale about us.

*LANDALL & GORDON*

*Joyners, Cabinet, & Chair - Makers*
*At ye Griffin & Chair in Little Argyle Street*
*by Swallow Street.*
*Makes all sorts of Tables, Chairs, Setee-Beds,*
*Looking-Glasses, Picture-frames, Window-*
*Blinds, & all sorts of Cabinet Work*

The trade card of Landall & Gordon, London cabinet-makers and
chair-makers, who were contemporaries of Thomas Chippendale. Their
place of business was at 'Ye Griffin & Chair'. *Circa* 1750. *Reproduced*
*by courtesy of the Trustees of the British Museum.*

# THE PLATES

The forty plates that follow are arranged in historical sequence, beginning with the simple boarded and joined furniture of the thirteenth century, and concluding with two examples of the 'contemporary' style. They have been selected to supplement the illustrations in the text, and, with their captions, form a survey of seven centuries of furniture design in England.

PLATE I   A thirteenth-century boarded oak chest; the simplest form of chest, raised slightly above ground level. The ledge with its hinged lid seen at one side, is to accommodate sweet-scented herbs such as lavender or dried woodruff. *Formerly in the collection of the late Robert Atkinson, F.R.I.B.A.*

PLATE II   Thirteenth-century oak chest with roundels of chip carving. Stated to have come from a church in Hampshire. *Reproduced by permission of the Victoria and Albert Museum, Crown copyright.*

PLATE III    An early sixteenth-century chest with a linen-fold motif carved on the front and side panels. *Reproduced by permission of the late R. W. Symonds.*

PLATE IV  A chest from Totnes, Devon, with different decorative
motifs carved on the front panels. Sixteenth century. *In the collection
of F. W. Wolsey, Esq. Below*: An elaborately carved chest, either late
sixteenth or early seventeenth century. The arcaded panels of the front
are separated by stiles carved in the form of caryatids which support
rudimentary versions of Ionic capitals. *Both illustrations are reproduced
by courtesy of the late R. W. Symonds.*

PLATE V  A mule chest in oak, showing the transition between the chest that was merely a box with a lid, and a more elaborate development that ultimately became the chest of drawers and the tallboy. Chests of this type were made at any time between 1640 and the end of the seventeenth century. *In the possession of the author. Below*: A Charles II chest in veneered walnut.

The decorative character depends on the use of oyster-wood veneering and cross-banding in sycamore on the edges of the panels, top, and drawer front. *Formerly in the collection of the late Robert Atkinson, F.R.I.B.A.*

Plate VI  Court cupboard of the early seventeenth century. *Reproduced by courtesy of the Victoria and Albert Museum, Crown copyright.*
*Below*: An oak draw-table, *circa* 1600, with bulbous legs, and Ionic capitals carved above the gadrooning on the bulbs. *Reproduced by courtesy of the Victoria and Albert Museum, Crown copyright.*

PLATE VII  A press cupboard in oak, dated 1610, with carved pilasters surmounted by Ionic capitals, flanking the central arcaded panel. This arcaded motif is repeated on the sides. The main supports are bulbous, with gadrooning on the upper part, and a crude representation of the acanthus leaf motif on the lower part. *Reproduced by courtesy of the Victoria and Albert Museum, Crown copyright.*

PLATE VIII  Oak dining table with a deep frieze carved with strapwork. The baluster legs are vase shaped. Dated 1697. From Hardwick Hall, Derbyshire. *Copyright, 'Country Life'.*

PLATE IX  Oak table with double gates, and ringed baluster legs and stretchers. *Circa* 1670. From Queen's College, Cambridge
*Copyright 'Country Life'.*

PLATE X    Oak double leaf gate-leg table, with barley sugar twist legs. *Circa* 1680. Modern ladderback rush-bottomed chair. *Formerly in the possession of the late Fleetwood Pritchard, Esq.*

*Below*: Double leaf gate-leg table with turned legs; and an early eighteenth-century settle with cabriole front legs.

PLATE XI    Double gate-leg table in oak, *circa* 1670–80. The legs are slender versions of Tuscan columns. Respect for architectural conventions is apparent, and the classic orders are already beginning to make an impact on furniture makers. *Below*: An eighteenth-century oak settle with a panel back. The front legs represent a crude attempt by the country craftsman to reproduce the cabriole leg and the ball foot. Compare this with the settle opposite, where a far more accomplished rendering of the cabriole leg has been achieved.

A joined armchair of oak, *circa* 1630, with incised carving on the back panel. *In the possession of Mrs. Grace Lovat Fraser.*

PLATE XII An oak joined chair, second quarter of the sixteenth century, with the linen-fold device used on the back and below the seat. The upper panel on the back is carved with Renaissance ornament. *Reproduced by courtesy of the Victoria and Albert Museum, Crown copyright.*

Turned and joined walnut chair, mid-seventeenth century. *Reproduced by courtesy of the Victoria and Albert Museum, Crown copyright.*

PLATE XIII    Carved and turned walnut armchair, *circa* 1670, with canework back and seat. The exuberant vitality and freedom of the carving celebrate the release from Puritan austerity. *Reproduced by courtesy of the Victoria and Albert Museum, Crown copyright.*

*Left*: A countrymade chair in walnut, with cabriole legs, turned stretchers and a rush seat, *circa* 1720. *In the author's possession.* *Right*: An oak writing chair of the same period. *In the possession of Julian Gloag, Esq.* The vase form is used for the back splats of both chairs.

PLATE XIV The salon at Houghton Hall, Norfolk. The interior decoration and furniture, 1730–35, were designed by William Kent. *Copyright 'Country Life'.*

PLATE XV A part of the painting by William Hogarth of the Assembly at Wanstead House, showing furniture by William Kent, and the highly decorative people who used it. Wanstead House was designed by Colin Campbell. The painting was probably finished in the fourth decade of the eighteenth century and was commissioned in 1727. *From the McFadden Collection in the Philadelphia Museum of Art.*

*Below*: A side table supporting a marble slab, designed by William Kent, showing a bold use of scrolls and classic motifs. From *Some Designs by Mr Inigo Jones and Mr Wm. Kent*, published by John Vardy, 1744.

PLATE XVI  Long-case clock in figured walnut, *circa* 1710–15.
The treatment of the hood suggests the influence of contemporary
architecture. The table is in Virginian walnut, a Queen Anne piece
with modified cabriole legs and hoof feet, lightly carved. The early
Georgian mirror frame is of walnut and gilt gesso. *From the collection
of the late Robert Atkinson, F.R.I.B.A*

PLATE XVII A cedar-lined press in mahogany, *circa* 1740. The swan-neck pediment, fluted pilasters, and cornice, all suggest the influence of architects on furniture design. The barometer, *circa* 1770, has a typical Hepplewhite twist in the base. *Formerly in the collection of the late Robert Atkinson, F.R.I.B.A.*

PLATE XVIII *Left*: Corner cupboard in oak, the pilasters, frieze and drawer fronts veneered in mahogany, inlaid with thin lines of boxwood and ebony. Made in the countryside, at any time between 1760 and 1790, it relies for its decorative effect on the varied colours of materials. *In the possession of Mrs. V. Atkins.*

*Below*: A mahogany chest, *circa* 1740–45, with carved cabriole legs and claw feet and one long drawer. *Formerly in the collection of the late Robert Atkinson, F.R.I.B.A.*

PLATE XIX  A serpentine-fronted mahogany chest, with fluted angles. The top drawer is fitted for use as a dressing or writing table. *Circa* 1740–50. The mirror has a mahogany frame, enriched with carved and gilded ornament. *Circa* 1730–40. *Formerly in the collection of the late Robert Atkinson, F.R.I.B.A.*

PLATE XX  A tallboy in mahogany. Architectural influence is visible in the fret on the frieze, and the cornice with dentals and the vertical flutes of the angles on the upper part. *Circa* 1740–50. The mirror on the right is early Georgian, with a mahogany frame and a swan-neck broken pediment: mouldings and carving are gilded. The chair, of Chippendale type, is carved in low relief. *Circa* 1760–70. Compare this with the ribbon-back chair shown on page 107. *Formerly in the collection of the late Robert Atkinson, F.R.I.B.A.*

PLATE XXI  A mahogany press, of the early Georgian period, with four cabriole, claw-footed legs on the base. This is one of the marks of a fine piece of furniture, for often the front legs only would be carved and finished with any elaboration. *Circa* 1725–30. The chair is later, about 1740, and in walnut, with carved shell ornament on the knees of the cabriole legs. *Formerly in the collection of the late Robert Atkinson, F.R.I.B.A.*

PLATE XXII    A bureau bookcase with a fall front escritoire drawer, and kneehole below. The use of large rectangular panes gave the name of 'sash-door' to this type of glazed door. *Circa* 1740–50. The chair on the right still retains some of the bold richness of the early Georgian period, especially in the cabriole legs. *Circa* 1735–45. *Formerly in the collection of the late Robert Atkinson, F.R.I.B.A.*

PLATE XXIII  A bed of Adam type, in kingwood, with a delicate twist on the front posts. The frieze has a Greek key pattern with a painted classical panel in the centre. *Circa* 1760. The mahogany press with drawers on the left, and the tripod table on the right, are of mid-eighteenth century origin. *Formerly in the collection of the late Robert Atkinson, F.R.I.B.A. Below*: A sideboard from Hepplewhite's *Guide*, 1787 edition. The classical influence of Robert Adam's work is apparent in this design.

PLATE XXIV   *Left*: A long-case clock in mahogany by John Godden of
Wingham. This is probably the John Godden of Town Malling (Wingham
is a few miles away), a clockmaker who worked in that part of Kent in the
late eighteenth century. *In the possession of Mrs. G. M. Gloag. Right*: A long-
case clock in mahogany with the hood surmounted by a swan-neck pediment. Like the clock by Godden, this was probably made at some time
during the last three decades of the eighteenth century.

PLATE XXV    A Chippendale gilt mirror, flanked by a pair of carved wood sconces with crystal drops, *circa* 1795. The grand piano is in dark satinwood by Josephus Merlin, London 1786. Two Battersea enamel candlesticks are used to light the keyboard and music, 1770. The music stand is of the Regency period in black and gilt, and the music canterbury behind it is painted and ornamented with flower decoration, *circa* 1800. A 'dummy board' of a dog is in the foreground. *In the collection of the late Sir Albert Richardson, P.P.R.A., at Avenue House, Ampthill.*

PLATE XXVI  Long-case clock in mahogany, stamped George
Augustus, and probably made for one of the royal palaces. *Circa*
1810. The chair is of the same period and the sphinx heads show
how Egyptian ornament, popularised by the work of Thomas Hope,
was beginning to affect English furniture design. *Formerly in the
collection of the late Robert Atkinson, F.R.I.B.A.*

PLATE XXVII An example of early nineteenth-century frivolity, probably based on a design by Thomas Hope. *Circa* 1810–15. The base is supported on dogs' heads, the table is of satinwood, partly polished, partly ebonized; the heads and feet of the figures are gilded, and the top is black marble. *Formerly in the collection of the late Robert Atkinson, F.R.I.B.A.*

PLATE XXVIII
*Above:* Three examples
of design in the Regency
style. Tea-caddy in rose-
wood: sewing-case in
birdseye maple inlaid with
brass, ebony and rose-
wood; and a silver christen-
ing mug.
*Right*: Early nineteenth-
century bookcase in satinwood with gilded brass
gallery on the upper
shelf. *In the possession of
Mrs. V. Atkins.*

PLATE XXIX  A sofa in black and gold, with a scroll end, covered in peach velvet. *Circa* 1805. In the collection at the Royal Pavilion, Brighton, South Drawing Room. *Reproduced by courtesy of the Brighton Art Gallery.*

PLATE XXX  A library table in dark mahogany cross-banded, with box lines. *Circa* 1800. A gilt scroll-back chair, decorated with carved acanthus leaves, with turned and reeded front legs, and swept back legs. *Circa* 1810. In the King's Bedroom of the Royal Pavilion at Brighton.

*Right*: One of four seats in the shape of a shell, supported by a dolphin, carved and gilded; probably part of the original furnishing of the Royal Pavilion. *Circa* 1805. *Both subjects reproduced by courtesy of the Brighton Art Gallery.*

PLATE XXXI  A circular library table on a fluted stem, decorated in gold, resting on a triangular base with carved and gilded paw feet. *In the King's Library at the Royal Pavilion, Brighton. Reproduced by courtesy of the Brighton Art Gallery.*

*Left*: A Regency chair in mahogany and a small tripod table of the same period. *Formerly in the possession of the late Mrs. Frances Evans.*

PLATE XXXII  *Left*: Early nineteenth-century Windsor chair, with turned legs and spur stretcher, in elm and yew. *Right*: Early nineteenth-century rush-seated chair, a rural craftsman's interpretation of a town fashion.

*Left*: Mid-Victorian papier-mâché chair in black with painted decoration and mother-of-pearl inlay. *Right*: Lady's chair with spoon back, black japanned frame, and upholstery of red Berlin wool background with multi-coloured bead embroidery. *Circa* 1850–60. *Formerly in the possession of Mrs. Grace Lovat Fraser.*

PLATE XXXIII   A library bookcase in mahogany with a broken front and attached Doric columns at the angles of the lower part, and arched glazed doors. *Circa* 1835–45. *In the possession of Bayliss, Jones & Bayliss Ltd., Wolverhampton.*

PLATE XXXIV  A davenport in walnut with carved, cabriole legs, supporting the desk. There is a rising nest of drawers, flanked by pigeon holes, and the desk slides forward. The drawer fronts are in satinwood. *Circa* 1845–50. *In the possession of Stanley Pollitt, Esq.*

PLATE XXXV   A walnut davenport with columns supporting the desk. The arms and crest depicted on the panel below are those of the family of Harris of Cructon (or Cruckton) in Shropshire. *Circa* 1835–45. *In the possession of Mrs. Alan Deller.*

Two davenports from Loudon's *Encyclopaedia* (1833), where they are spelt devonport, and described as 'drawing-room writing-cabinets used by ladies'. (Figs. 1945 and 1946, page 1066.)

PLATE XXXVI  *Right*: A bedside bookcase in mahogany with drawers, designed and made by Ernest Gimson.

*Below*: A sideboard designed in 1929 by Sir Ambrose Heal. Veneered in walnut with a veneered sycamore interior.

PLATE XXXVII  A sideboard and table in Englsh walnut, designed by
Sir Gordon Russell. Compare this with the chests on Plate IV and the
mule chest on Plate V: they are in the same tradition of design, though
the twentieth-century designer knows far more about choosing and
handling wood, and the subtleties of decoration. The notching of the
chamfers on the foot of the modern sideboard has satisfied the modern
designer, who has used fielded panels on the cupboard doors to empha-
sise, by the play of light and shade, the rich colour and figuring of the wood.

PLATE XXXVIII    Artist-craftsmen like Ernest Gimson (1864–
1919) revived the spirit of the native English style, and their work was
related to that of the Puritan and pre-Renaissance English craftsmen.
They had nothing in common with the master cabinet makers and
carvers of the Queen Anne and Georgian periods. This cabinet in
figured English walnut was made in Ernest Gimson's own workshop
about 1918.

PLATE XXXIX A dressing table, toilet mirror, pair of candlesticks and a stool of English walnut, designed in the early nineteen-twenties, by Sir Gordon Russell.

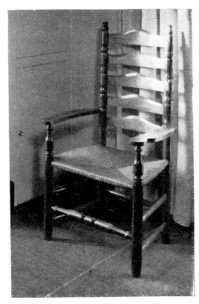

Two ladder-back rush-seated chairs. *Left*: Oak chair, designed and made by Ernest Gimson. *Right*: Chair in yew designed and made by Sir Gordon Russell. (See also chair on plate X.)

PLATE XL Furniture in
the 'contemporary' style
of the late nineteen-fifties
and early nineteen-sixties.
*Right*: Sideboard designed
by A. J. Milne for Heal
& Son Ltd.

*Below*: Group of unit
furniture, which may be
arranged in various ways
and supplemented by
other pieces. Designed by
R. C. Heritage for G. W.
Evans Ltd. *Reproduced
from Design in British
Industry, by courtesy of the
author, Michael Farr.*

# INDEX

Where page numbers are given in italics, thus *137*, they refer to a caption.

Bobbin turning, 3, 50, 55, 60
Bookcases, 18, 84, 94, 108, 112, *136*, 153
Bookshelves, 100
Boxwood, 108
Brackets, 100
Brackett, Oliver, 167
Bradley, Edward (Cuthbert Bede), 143
*Brave New World*, 156
Bridgens, Richard, *xvi*, *15*
Bronze furniture, 20, 74, 150, 155
Brown, Ford Madox, 119
Buffet stool, 43
Bureaux, 16, 68, 75, 86, 97
Bureau-bookcases, 75, 153, 158
Burlington, Richard Boyle, third earl of, 78, 84, 86
Burne-Jones, Sir Edward, 119
Burr-elm, 133

*Cabinet and Chair-Maker's Real Friend and Companion, The*, 101
*Cabinet Dictionary, The*, 19, 106, *143*
*Cabinet Maker, and Art Furnisher, The*, *137, 138, 139*
*Cabinet-Maker and Upholsterer's Drawing-Book, The*, 106, *142*
*Cabinet-Maker and Upholsterer's Guide; or a Repository of Designs for every article of Household Furniture, The*, *111*, 167
*Cabinet-Makers' and Upholsterers' Guide, Drawing Book, and Repository of New and Original Designs for Household Furniture*, *123*, 167
*Cabinet-Maker's Guide, or Rules and Instructions in the art of varnishing, dying, staining, japanning, polishing, lackering and beautifying Wood, Ivory, Tortoiseshell, and Metal, The*, *xv*
*Cabinet-Maker, Upholsterer, and General Artist's Encyclopaedia, The*, 106
Cabinets, 16, 18, 57, 65, 67-70, 77, 86, 108, 133, 153
Cabinet-stands, 18, 60, 65, 67, 68, 70, 74
Cabriole leg, 17, 18, 20, 21, 62, 67, 71, 73, 74, 79, 86, 96, 129

Cane-work, 59, 60, 62, 63, 70, 75, 102, *103*, 112, *140*
Carving, 35, 49, 56, 59, 65, 87, *103*, *123*, *137*
chip, 40, 45
early Georgian, 18
gouge, *3*
Grinling Gibbons' decorative, 76
linen-fold, 41, 45
modern fake, 17
scroll, *3*
tracery, *3*, 40, 41
*Cassell's Household Guide*, *140*
Casson, Sir Hugh and Lady, 156
Cassone, 40
Cast iron, *146, 148*, 149
Cescinsky, Herbert (quoted), 39
*Chairmakers' Guide, The*, 101
Chairs, 16, 20-22, 41-43, *45*, 47-48, 49, 50-51, 56, 60, 61, 62, 63, 64, 66-67, 70, 71, 72-73, 75, 86, 87, 89, 95-96, *103*, 105, 110, 116, 117-118, 133
Adam, 87, 102
balloon-back, 117, *141*
cane-seated, 63, *140*
cast-iron, *146, 148*
Chippendale, 87, 95-96, *107*
coffer-maker's, *36*, 48
conversation, *143*
country-made, 55, 64
drawing-room, *123*
elbow, 79
folding, *140*
'Gothic', *146*
'Grandfather', 61
Hepplewhite, 87, 110, 111
ladder-back, 87, 96
lug, 61
metal, *147, 148*, 150
'Quaint', *139, 140*
Queen Anne, 17, 75
reading, *142*
'Ribband back', *107*
rocking, *141*
Sheraton, 20, *103*, 110, *142, 143*
shield-back, 87, 101, 102, 110, *111*
single, *3*, 60
smoker's, *142*
steel, 31, 42
turned, *3*

Elizabethan furniture, 7, 8, 44, 46
Elm, 32, 78, 133
*England under Queen Anne* (quoted), 13
'English Empire', 112
*English Furniture from Charles II to George II*, 90, (quoted), 94
English Renaissance, 6, 8, 12
Evelyn, John, 11, 13, 76, (quoted), 12, 52, 58, 64, 70

Farr, Michael, 172
'Farthingale' chairs, 44, *49*
Fern-stands, 28
Filing cabinets, 151
Fireplaces, 60, 61
Firescreens, 100
Fitzwilliam Museum, Cambridge, *3*
Flemish influence, 51
Fletcher, Sir Banister, 171
Fonthill Abbey, 99
French Empire furniture, 20, 21, 74, 110
French influence, 17, 20, 21, 84, 110
Fry, E. Maxwell, 156
Fry, Roger, 86, (quoted), 88, 118
*Furniture and Decoration and the Furniture Gazette*, 140, 141, 142
Furniture:
bronze, 20, 74
Commonwealth, 10, 12, 47, 48, 50, 52-54, 56, 58
Edwardian, 86, 88
Elizabethan, 7, 8, 44, 46
French Empire, 20, 21, 74, 110
Georgian, 18, 19, 78, 79, *83*, 116
'Jaco', 51, 129, 161
Mediaeval, 5, 6, 37, 38, 39, 40, 41
modern (in the English tradition), 30, 32, 136, 163
modern (revolutionary), 30, 31, 32, 150-151, 152
papier-mâché, 117
Queen Anne, 16-18, 30, 72, 74, 75, 129
Regency, *103*
Roman, 20, 74, 110
steel, 2, 31, 42, 48, 149, 151, 152, 153, 154, 155
Stuart (early), 7, 8, 48, 51
Stuart (late), 58, 67, 69, 75
Tudor, 41, 43, 44

Furniture—*contd*.
Victorian, 8, 27, 28, 116, 117, 150
William and Mary, 65, 69, 75
*Furniture from Machines* (quoted), 155-156
*Furniture with Candelabra and Interior Decoration*, xvi

Gadrooning, *3*, 86
Gate-legged tables, 52, 55, 72
*Genteel Household Furniture in the Present Taste*, 100
*Gentleman and Cabinet Maker's Director, The*, 99, *107*, *145*, (quoted), 95
George I, 77, 78
Georgian furniture, 18, 19, 78, 79, *83*, 116
Germany, 74
Gesso, 76, 77, *83*
Gibberd, Sir Frederick, 156, **171**
Gibbons, Grinling, 76, 77
Gibbs, James, 75
Gilding, 18, 20, 21, 57, 67, *83*, 86, 90, *91*, 104
Gillow, Richard, 101
Gimson, Ernest, 29, 32, *114*, 126, 130-135, 154, 155, 171, (quoted), 133
Girandoles, 100
Glass, 150, 153, 154, 155
Gothic revival, 115-117, *144*
Gothic taste, 19, *146*
Gramophones, 33
'Grandfather' chair, 61
*Graphic, The*, *141*
Greek revival, 20, 21, 110, 112
Green, Romney, 126, 130
Gribble, Ernest, 169

Hampton Court, 44, 77
Hawksmoor, Nicholas, 75
Heal, Sir Ambrose, 32, *114*, 128, 135, 154, 169
Heart-shaped back, *87*
Henry VII, 6
Henry VIII, 6
Hepplewhite, A. & Co., *111*, 167
Hepplewhite, George, 22, 30, 61, *87*, 97, 101, 102, 106, 110, *111*, 132, 168
High Wycombe, 117, 118, 130

# INDEX

THE END